FIGURES IN
A BYGONE LANDSCAPE

Don Haworth was educated at Burnley Grammar School,
served in the Royal Air Force and worked as a journalist in
print and radio in several parts of the world. He joined the
BBC as a television news reporter, worked on *Tonight* and
Panorama and then became a documentary producer based
in Manchester. His film *Fred Dibnah, Steeplejack*, won a
British Academy Award in 1980. His work as a playwright
has been primarily for radio; the plays have been broadcast
in many parts of the world and three have won Giles
Cooper Awards in the past eight years. *Figures in a Bygone
Landscape* was the winner of the 1986 Portico Prize.

'One aspect of the book that pleased me particularly was
the author's refusal to exaggerate or satirise; its interest
requires no tarting up, a process far too common in
accounts of bygone days.' Roy Fuller

'He remembers his young life with wry humour, insight
and a sharp recall which brings the era to life.' *Manchester
Evening News*

'The prose is seamless, the recollections benevolent and
astute.' *The Guardian*

'Vivid, funny and marvellously perceptive . . . His book is
a delight.' *Cheshire Life*

DON HAWORTH

FIGURES
IN A
BYGONE LANDSCAPE

❧❀❧

A
LANCASHIRE CHILDHOOD

With line drawings by
Roy Newton

A Methuen Paperback

A Methuen Paperback
First published in Great Britain 1986
Reprinted 1986 (twice), 1987
This paperback edition published 1987
by Methuen London Ltd, 11 New Fetter Lane
London EC4P 4EE
© 1986 by Don Haworth
Printed in Great Britain
by Cox & Wyman Ltd, Reading

British Library Cataloguing in Publication Data

Haworth, Don
Figures in a bygone landscape : a
Lancashire childhood.——(A Methuen
                paperback).
1. Lancashire——Social life and customs
                I. Title
942.7′6084   DA670.L2

ISBN 0-413-17080-2

To my mother

CONTENTS

1 · EARLY EXPLORATIONS

The council house where I was born in 1924 in Clover Street, Bacup, was on a small new estate in the shade of old trees. The carts and delivery vans of tradesmen made the sound and smell of morning, the snort of horses, the grind and joggle of spoked wheels, the rat-tat of knockers, men whistling, the smell of horse muck and of fallen vegetables slippery to the heel.

I learned that God watched over this daily bustle as an extension to his job of watching over me. He had button eyes and red trousers and perched on my cot. By the time the distinction was made between God and Golliwog the image was ineradicable so that later efforts to grasp the concept of the Trinity or the immanent and emergent god of the life force always wilted under the grin of Robertson's doll. Now his name has been pared in deference to the Race Relations Act I can capture a glimpse of Nietzsche's concept of an expiring God.

A doctor came and put me through it. He was called Dr Brown, which was obviously an alias. He looked like photographs of Marcel Proust with a black moustache and sleeked hair and unblinking eyes. He thrust a spoon into my throat which rattled on my teeth, and sat in an upright chair threatening not to go until I stopped crying. He left some evil dark medicine, distilled from his name, which gave me whooping cough. My mother lit a fire in the bedroom at night and perched God on the cot rail and sang me to sleep. When she had gone downstairs coals fell out of the grate and set the oilcloth on fire. She emptied hot water bottles on the flames and the room filled with steam. I went to sleep on her knee in the living room and woke on my father's knee. I cannot remember seeing him before that. In the bedroom he knelt and passed his hands over the charred oilcloth to show it was no longer hot.

It was a pleasure to watch his hands and his bare arms when he was at work, particularly hand-stitching a shoe. He would sit with it between his knees, turn it, pierce the welt with an awl, draw the thread long and tug it tight in a fluent pattern of movement that caused my chest to tighten and left me ready to sleep. He had machines in the room above his shop, a finisher and a carborundum wheel that threw flecks on to his face. There was an open trap in the floor so he could see anybody who came into the shop. The place smelt of leather and beeswax and shoe polish. I knew that to be allowed to go anywhere away from home was a reward for merit. Going to his shop every day was evidence of his great virtue.

I tried to follow his example. Clover street is up by the cricket field steeply above the town centre. The journey would have to begin down a flight of steps behind the houses where I had been forbidden to venture beyond a token piece of string stretched across the top landing. My mother lived in fear of accidents. Already I had nearly gone up in smoke in the bedroom, reins intended to restrain me from darting under the wheels of carts had snapped and I had fallen and broken my teeth, and she was aware of the ever-present danger in the shop of my being carried round by the belting on the machinery and tossed through the trap in the floor. Her fear of the steps was so vividly conveyed that my memory of them reeling down into the mist of the morning like an illustration to a fairy story has not in the least been corrected by the discovery years later of a flight in their place little more than a single storey high. I descended and was rewarded by being made the centre of drama after recapture. I conducted parties of children to the bottom where we waited to watch ashen faces cluster on the landing above. I lost the companionship of the twins Joan and Brian Hargreaves who on return from their travels were confined to barracks. My cousin Stanley Kerry was held up as an example as he tricycled in a circle round the garden. Dr Brown spoke to me and made me cry. The Reverend Bert Matthews urged a localized life in kindlier terms. Crones from the chapel dredged up from their race memory remedies to bind the body and break the spirit. I was threatened with and finally apprehended by the policeman, but he gave me a sweet on the way back and thus added himself to the incentives to travel. Eventually I made it all the way to my father's shop and beyond that to my grandmother Haworth's house where he parked me for safety. It was the cavern of delight that lies at the end of every epic journey.

My own home was bare with hard light and separate objects of furniture. In the hall an aspidistra grew in a brass pot on a high and not too stable pedestal. More vegetation spurted from a vase which stood on a circular mirror on a plush cloth in the centre of the dining room table, a solid oak job wrought jointly as a wedding present by grandfather Haworth and uncle Ben Kerry. They had also made the dining chairs which stood back on the oilcloth against the walls and the magnificent sideboard, in whose large plate mirror we were multiplied to infinity through the mirror on the mantlepiece opposite.

My grandmother Haworth's home rested the eyes and the heart. It was indeed a cavern, a still dark room, with only one way in, so doors could not unexpectedly open, and a window overcast by the buildings opposite so the light of day died early. The objects all belonged together like the features of a harmonious landscape and emerged to separate sight only after a little time. Two white pot policemen and three white pot dogs stood guard along the shelf above the great iron fire range. You heard movement; the cat stepped from the corner cupboard and kittens fell back off her into the darkness. The fire sang and the wall clock beat and my grandmother in a rocking chair topped and tailed gooseberries or peeled apples or shelled peas which she dropped into pans and colanders on the rag rug at her feet. She was not like us. She was a countrywoman, though she had left her Norfolk village as a child and worked all her life in the mills. She did not speak much, and never in exhortation or reproof. The room was full of peace. It smelt of fruit and gravy.

Grandma Haworth gave me money to buy sweets at Mr Lord's shop opposite the big cotton mill in Burnley road. With her I could get away with buying kali, a white powder, otherwise called sherbet, which came in a yellow cardboard cylinder about three inches long and was sucked out through a tube of liquorice inserted in the top. In judicious quantities it fizzed pleasantly on the tongue, but it was easy to draw in such a draught that a blob of the stuff hit the back of the throat. Children would cough and retch, go purple, writhe on the floor and drum their heels. It gave kali a bad name. Unlike other adults, my grandmother did not exhort me to renounce the addiction. She let me suck in peace at the liquorice tube which soon melted and blocked, and when I gave up to it, not having met more intelligent children who knew about breaking into the container with scissors, she would pick it up as though she had just noticed it and ask, 'Have you finished?' and throw it on the fire. Its explosion lit the room.

It was an interesting place to go for a pee. My grandmother would reach down the key which hung by the fire range at the foot of one of the pot policemen and we would cross the front yard to the water closet. It was shared with several families and kept locked so it should not be accessible to the public at large. The ladies of the families took turns in cleaning it and maintained in pride and competition a standard suited to an operating theatre. It reeked of disinfectant. The walls were whitewashed, the boards scrubbed pale, the floor done in two colours of rubbing stone. Newspaper torn into neat squares hung on a string. Some closets were even equipped with the Manchester Guardian. When my grandmother lifted the wooden cover from over the hole flies came up like a box barrage and with them the warm sweet smell of the sewer. If the door was left open to let in light you could see the ripple across the bottom of the deep shaft. There was then the matter of refraining from wetting the boards. She tried holding me aloft, standing me on bricks and buckets and finally hoisted me to stand astride the hole. 'Where would I go if I fell down?' I asked. She was a placid woman, not to be troubled by an overwrought imagination. 'You mun take care and not fall down,' she said.

I made sure of getting this visit over before my grandfather came home from work. In my time he was a genial and kindly man, much mellowed, but he remained gruff and rough and his heavy hands were clumsy with children's buttons. I knew to expect him when other home-bound workers passed the window and clattered up the stone steps that led to the next terrace. Most of them glanced in and spoke a passing greeting in the lip language they used in the mills, women in black cotton and clogs, pale men in faded boiler suits. Some would wrench open the door and dump a parcel or shout something brisk. A little woman noticed me with a swivel of her spectacle lenses that reflected several segments of eyes. 'Art thou Archie's?' she said. 'Con he speak?' she asked my grandmother. 'He can speak,' my grandmother said. 'He never stops'. The woman caught me by the arm. She needed a shave. 'Thou mun't be feared of strangers, cock. Thou mun oppen thi mouth.'

With my grandfather I learned to hit off the right idiom. I saw he was not a client for piping verbosities. 'Thou'rt here again, art thou?', he would ask, and I would say 'Aye'. 'What hast thou been up to?', he would ask, and I would say 'Nowt'. He would chuckle and settle in and the calm closed again over the ripples caused by his arrival. He smoked a pipe. He prodded down the glow in the bowl with his forefinger on which the nail damaged in an accident grew like a claw. I was startled to discover that what he smoked was dog muck. He unscrewed the lid of his tobacco tin and there it was nestling at the bottom. He called it twist, and sometimes when he ran out he sent me to Mr Lord's for a further consignment. 'Tell him to put a jockey on it', he said, which made sense to Mr Lord because when he had weighed out the tobacco on his brass scale he cut off another small turd which he dropped on top. 'There's his jockey.'

My grandfather prepared his pipe at leisure, blowing through it, shaking the stem hissing into the fire, then rolling the twist between his palms into loose light strands to pack into the bowl. Its quickening glow reflected on the walls and ceiling and the room filled with rolling smoke. He did everything on a lavish scale. Coal he threw on the fire a bucketful at a time. The room went dark, then the slack exploded and the cobbles caught and flames roared up the great throat of the chimney. Across the yard on his small raised garden he maintained a forest of sooty rhubarb carpeted with mint. He would fell a swathe, wrenching the sticks up and tossing them into a heap in the yard. 'Take that home to thi mother when thou goes.'

The rhubarb was received with due excitement and gratitude and his name honoured each day that stewed rhubarb or a rhubarb pie appeared on the table. It was more than we could get through. Smaller bundles were made up and delivered about the estate, to my other grandparents the Sephtons and their neighbour Archie Slater the Bacup cricket professional, to our cousins the Kerrys a few doors away, to our neighbour Mrs Yates who disappointed me by refusing to give some to her cat, and to an evasive old man who was suspected of turning the good fruit into alcohol. All these people had little clumps of rhubarb in their new gardens but nothing that would ever compare with the great canopy of grandfather Haworth's plantation.

I discovered through visiting my grandparents another brood that belonged to us. My uncle Frank's family lived in Fern street in a terrace so steep that I could not understand how their toy train could stay on its track instead of toppling into the wall and, although I saw that everybody was straight and level while I was there, the impression remained of a family constantly toiling against the gradient of their floor. My cousin Evelyn, who was a year older than I, had the child's face of grandmother Haworth. Her brother, six weeks my junior, I thought of with pity as what we would learn to call an underprivileged child. It was not only the canted floor; he had no proper name. He had been dubbed Carlton in memory of his mother's brother killed in the war, but the name was felt to be too outrageous to use. He was addressed by everyone, however junior as the years went by, as Sonny. An even greater disability came to light.

He had no proper birthday or, if he had, only at appalling intervals, having been born on the 29th of February. The sum of his misfortunates was so overpowering that it swamped any other memory of him in these early years.

My auntie Nellie addressed us all as 'cock'. She spoke the same curt and broad speech I fell into with my grandfather, and this seemed odd. Most mothers spoke in a different way which reached a peak of refinement when they read from story books. The people on our council estate 'talked nicely'. It went with pebble dash and with not wearing shawls or walking whippets. Some would drop into the old speech in talking to aged relatives or in shouting in anger at boys. My grandfather Sephton whose native speech was less broad than that of East Lancashire would drop into it when he wished to emphasize the simple honesty and wholesomeness of his attitudes or of what he was talking about. It is possible that the distinctions of speech might not have been readily perceptible to the outside ear, to visitors say from outer space or Guildford. The degree of change was limited to what could be managed naturally. Beyond that it was considered affectation, 'talking posh', which was acceptable only in doctors and clergymen and those schoolteachers known not to be local in origin. Our little council estate was, I suppose, among the first forward positions occupied by the working class in its historic advance to Acacia Avenue.

We were soon winkled out. The whole family of us, ourselves, the Kerrys, the grandparents Sephton, began a retreat which continued with long delaying actions and brief counter-attacks until I was grown up. The council houses were too expensive. The estate had been built as a sort of show-piece, the first in the district of the 'homes for heroes' promised at the end of the war. To live there was generally considered not so much heroic as downright reckless, a wild squandering of good money on such frivolities as a bathroom and a patch of garden. The rent at sixteen shillings a week amounted to a third of what my father earned and was more than double what a house in the streets would cost. It became too much to find. Grandfather Sephton's income from his insurance work was falling, and the costs of the other two families, ourselves and the Kerrys, were rising with the birth to each of a second child in 1927, my brother Eric and my cousin Margaret.

2 · UP THE VALLEY

We went to live at Troughgate, at 1,000 feet the highest point in the moorland valley between Bacup and Rochdale. The house, two rooms upstairs and two down, was in the stone terraces that straddled narrowly along between the road and the railway. My parents regarded our retreat there as temporary, my father having prepared to launch himself into an executive career by taking a job as a branch manager at Burnley Co-op. I do not know whether he felt regret at giving up his little shop. The general wisdom of the time saw God on the side of the big battalions. It seemed a necessary step. With the proceeds of his business he bought a BSA motor bike and travelled over to Burnley each day. We saw little of him through the week except on nights when snow was falling and my mother spun out our preparations for bed so as not to wait alone. She sang and read stories, but sometimes she could not concentrate and she closed the book and we waited. We would hear the note of the stopping engine and my father would appear at the threshold, the whirling night behind him, like an enormous snowman.

The house was next door to a potato pie shop and permanently enveloped in its aroma. Other sustaining smells came and went: the burning of winter grass when the moors crackled and flared under columns of smoke, the smell of spring before poison sprays when thousands of flowers brightened the hedgerows and meadows, the tang of coal tar brought in a horse-drawn boiler and dribbled by men with buckets between the cobbles of the road. On hot days a ghost of the smell arose again when the tar melted. Infants poked at it with sticks and coated themselves so they looked like zebras. They were cuffed, rubbed with lard to emulsify the tar and rasped with the scrubbing brush. Their friends gathered round the door to hear them howl.

The railway ran behind the houses in a cutting, so that from the moors opposite the steam cloud seemed to creep along without cause or support like a moving geyser. At the sound of a train children on the back street swarmed up the fence of railway sleepers and the engine driver, seeing the line of peering heads sounded his whistle and sometimes as a special treat cleared the boiler, blasting fire and cinders from the funnel in a terrifying roar that left us deafened and chastened in a gently falling shower of damp soot.

I had no doubt that we had fallen on a fuller life. The motor bike alone was evidence of that. It stood on the road outside the front door, and passers-by of all ages stopped to admire it and occasionally to work the fittings, the gear lever at the side of the petrol tank, the brass pump mounted on top by which the rider squirted oil round the works, the clutch, throttle, mixture and ignition control levers, and the bulb horn which everybody felt free to hoot. It smelled of petrol and leather and vegetable oil, a fragrance that lulled and lifted the spirit like divine grace or a June garden. When my father kicked up the engine, window panes rattled and assemblies of persons suddenly appeared as though they had materialized out of the exhaust cloud. I sometimes travelled short distances behind him, fingers dug hard into the sides of his overcoat, head pressed against the swell of his back, eyes down watching the sets of the road ripple past, scared stiff.

At first I was not admitted to the company of the boys who played on the cinder back street. They took issue with my costume. They wore clogs and cut-down trousers and big cloth caps which harmonised well with the landscape, and they were appalled by my outlandish Sunday ensemble, fashioned by a ladies' dressmaker, of a waistcoat and short trousers of brown velvet worn over a cream blouse with a matching straw hat. They howled and set upon me. Afterwards whenever I tried to climb the fence of railway sleepers to watch trains pass they would come and tug me down. I was no longer wearing the velvet suit but I understood this was a life sentence for an offence beyond retraction or atonement. At the sound of a train they would swarm up the fence, clogs clattering against the boards, and dispatch a flunkey to incommode me, usually an idiot or a small child without trousers whom I could repel but not shake off in time. I decided to try to see by digging under the fence with the coal shovel. They came and sneered at the hole and eventually their ringleader Sam White kicked the heap of cinders back into it. I rounded. They fled. I saw the billowing crown of Sam White's segmented cloth cap and brought the shovel down on the centre button.

His mother came to our front door, a big woman wearing a black cotton skirt in which small children clung. She did not complain but established fact. 'Have you a little lad called Donald? Well, he's hit our little lad over th' head wi' a shovel. He's laid out cold on t' sofa.' She returned some hours later to report him still comatose. Crones came and peered round the jamb of the door at me. Persons arrived, quietly stated their relationship with the victim, and departed. My poor mother had no idea how to respond. The absence of moralizing, the lack of any expression of grief or outrage, left her at a loss. She did not understand that it was their sufficient purpose merely to stake a claim to a part in the melancholy drama. She did her best. She sent Sam White a custard to speed his recuperation and issued an amendment to standing orders. Never again must I take the shovel out of the yard. Henceforth I should have to make my way through life with a wooden spade.

On the road which passed the front door a tram came every hour and five or six motor cars. Motorists were deadly. They downed pedestrians as though they were competing in a heartless sport. There was nothing much wrong with the cars, Austin Sevens and bullnosed Morrises, but many of the drivers were unacquainted with machinery or used to machines of a different order such as stationary steam engines and colliery winding gear. It was nothing in the course of a short journey to uproot the handbrake, de-knob the gear shift and wrench off a fistful of levers. People in those days were born with heavy hands and unco-ordinated feet. Some never learned to waddle them on the pedals. Others had to mumble drills and watch the antics of their boots. By the time they looked up again another pedestrian was disappearing under the bonnet.

'Mind t' motors,' parents would call as a parting word, and with good reason. I believe there were nearly as many road accidents in the late 'twenties as there are today with only a twentieth of the traffic and a speed limit, until 1930, of 20 m.p.h. From half a mile away in an empty road a car would home in on a person as relentlessly as a guided missile, and that was not the end. People did not speak of being knocked down but of being run over, which provokes a dreadful vision of drivers, unable either to stop or swerve, downing their victim then bump, bump, straight over him.

The steam traction engine with its train usually of two carts was a more frightening vehicle. We would hear its pounding beat and see its column of black smoke over the brow of the road, then it came to full view, rumbling over the cobbles, rattling teeth and windows, the driver peering round the flywheel, his face black with oil from the exposed piston. It was terrifying, but not nearly so dangerous as the motor cars whose drivers sailed past white at the knuckles and with teeth clenched. Mr Pollard from Shawforth just down the road got out for a rest when he made it as far as Troughgate. He was a big man with a kindly but flustered red face. He raised his hat to the crones sitting in the doorways, releasing from his matted hair a small cloud of steam which rose parallel to the column from the radiator. 'I'm getting on top of it,' he would say, 'I'm mastering it, slowly'.

'Thee take thi time, Jo. Rome weren't built in a day.'

He had not been christened Jo but at some time when his name had been written on an exercise book or a shop sign, Pollard, someone had amended it to Jo Lard. This gentle, slightly pathetic name and his apologetic demeanour distinguished him from the normal run of desperadoes at the wheel. Indeed he was so concerned not to be carried away into uncontrollable speed that he could hardly get started.

'Petrol, Jo, petrol,' his instructor shouted as the car juddered to a stop. He was the garage man and the instruction was thrown in as part of the purchase price. They were both big men wearing overcoats and hats and so tightly crammed into the little car that Mr Pollard scarcely had elbow room to wrestle with the wheel. When he succeeded in letting in the clutch the pace so alarmed him that the garage man had to get a tackle in, football style, to keep the throttle open. They came to grief on a hill start. After umpteen failures the garage man jammed the accelerator open, Mr Pollard in panic brought his boot down on the clutch and with the disengaged engine roaring they rolled slowly backwards into a greengrocer's shop. Apples and turnips bounced down the pavement. Customers spoke rebukes. Mr Pollard renounced the motor car.

A more persistent learner downed our friend Peter Pilling shortly after his fourth birthday. The accident was sufficiently modish for the family to take some pride in it, more especially when he was returned from Rochdale Infirmary so completely swathed in bandages that it looked as though they were taking delivery of a roll of linoleum. The house became a public attraction like a booth at a fun fair. Peter's mother sat at the front door admitting us in small parties. His grandfather, taking on shape in the curtained darkness, named aloud the gifts we added to a mound of chocolate, books and small toys at the sofa head. Peter rumbled thanks from inside his cylinder.

Accidents of all sorts abounded. Mrs Fruin, auntie Abbie's washerwoman, trapped her fingers in the mangle then fell down the cellar steps and broke her arm. I pulled my father's motor bike over on top of me. He was knocked off it on his way back from Burnley at night in a snow storm. A green Todmorden corporation motor bus skidded over the edge on the same moorland road. My mother and I made the journey in another bus the following Saturday. Few of the passengers could bring themselves to look down into the snow-filled gullies; some prayed with silent moving lips. I understood this. Life was fraught with danger, and the best safeguard was to cultivate the friendship of Jesus. We had a whip-round for him every week at Sunday school. We trooped round and poked our pennies into a box held by a child who had a birthday in the past or coming week and who could be trusted not to drop the box or make a pool. While the lesson proceeded we could hear the box being jemmied open by a young man in plus-fours at the back of the room. He wrapped up columns of pennies in small sheets torn from a church magazine, and went out to deliver them. We wondered how that was done. We knew he would not be able to hand them over to Jesus personally, and we were worried lest some chain of adults, as gormless as our teacher when we inquired about it, should deliver the parcel to the wrong address. God lived in the chapel next door and we did not want him to collar the money. He was frightening. He could see you under the table. He knew everything you did or thought. For two pins he would come down on you like a ton of bricks. Jesus was a different cup of tea. He had a kindly face, performed tricks and had been extensively photographed with lambs, donkeys and multi-racial infants. For a consideration he would fend God off and not have you sunk at sea. That is why it was specified that he should have the whole of the collection. We sang:

Dropping, dropping, dropping, dropping, hear the pennies fall.
Every one for Jesus, he shall have them all.

Moreover money contributed to Jesus's stipend was not entirely down the drain. There was a hinted prospect of a rebate.

Now that we are little, pennies are in store,
But when we get older, we shall have them more.
Dropping, dropping, dropping, dropping, hear the pennies fall.
Every one for Jesus, he shall have them all.

For my own part I needed to keep in well with Jesus because God had me taped for a number of specific crimes and also for daily infraction of rules which were largely made known in retrospect. My mother had been brought up in the country in a religious family of girls. She was not accustomed to males nor to a rough district. My behaviour often grieved and disappointed her. She conveyed that I was a disappointment to Jesus too. They both took it badly when I threw wooden building blocks at my brother's head for leaning out from his high chair and cuffing my Hornby train from the table to the floor. Some time later he won a prize at a baby show for being fat which at first was reassuring but on reflection led to concern lest his head might be inflating at a disproportionate rate. It gave us an interest for several years to see whether he would grow up idiotic.

It was a cosy house especially on dark evenings when rain swept over the moors and battered the windows or when the outside world lay so muted under fallen snow that indoor sounds could be heard from several houses away. We were washed in a zinc bath in front of the fire, screened by a wooden maiden on which towels were put to warm. Eric went in first and I was trained to stand ready with a towel as he was lifted pink and dripping from the water. We laid him on the table, dusted him with white powder, then turned him and sprinkled the other side as though he was a piece of liver. He was then taken up to his cot and it was my turn for the bath which was warmed up with a ladling can of water from the boiler by the fire. The bath bottom was slippery and pleasantly yielding, coated with a deposit of soap and lime from the water. My mother left me in my pyjamas in front of the fire and I heard the bump and gurgle as she emptied the bath into the stone slopstone and hung it on the wall. I had some supper and she sang or read a story. I said my prayers on her knee:

Gentle Jesus, meek and mild, look upon a little child.
Pity my simplicity. Suffer me to come to thee.

It served to fortify or after a sinful day to restore my friendship with Jesus. Some nights, as I have said, she allowed me to stay up until my father arrived; he was away more than twelve hours and they were long days for her alone with two young children and among neighbours she did not yet understand. But there was an ease about the district and it grew on her. We were happy there in the warm enveloping aroma from Chesney's potato pie shop next door. On Fridays we took our yellow enamel dish and captured a pie.

I awoke early on Christmas morning aware of a presence in the room besides my brother in his cot. A giant with a great round head was standing over my bed. I ducked under the clothes and must have gone to sleep because when I peeped out the gas was lighted and my mother was lifting Eric from his cot. A bolster-full of Christmas presents stood by my bed with a football perched on top. It was a small but real leather football. The whole district came to revolve around it. Boys came up from Shawforth and down from hill farms to swell the throng who fought and hacked to get a toe to the ball on the cinder back street between the yard walls and the sleeper fence. Clogs fastened only by a clasp flew in the air. Boys fell in writhing heaps. The ball scarcely moved. It was more like traditional football as played by Etonians and yokels. At one moment all the players would be flailing in, the next everybody gone as suddenly as though a drain had swallowed them. They were back just as suddenly. A dateless old man popped out of his back gate like a figure on a weathercock and announced to nobody 'They're playing football again'. An unconcerned woman in another gate said aimiably by way of greeting to any adult who emerged 'It drives you distracted'.

Dogs were predictable. Some watched with a single open eye from the coal place roof when you went into their yard to retrieve the ball, others raised a harmless storm of barking and chain-rattling, and one, a red setter, sank his teeth. Adults were beyond reckoning up. One day, perhaps if a visitor was present, they would welcome you in with a show of kindly indulgence; the next they would impound the ball. Individually they might take no notice. Together they set each other off, like Zulus on the eve of battle, working up from indignation to bellicose abuse, then to a frontal attack aimed first at extracting their own children, then broadening as the frenzy increased to a general assault on all footballers. They would subside into sanity and, half ashamed, justify their brainstorm. 'Most of you don't live on this back street.' The weathercock man would repeat a searching legalistic point. 'If they tumble over the top, who's liable?' This had to do with getting into yards usually of people out at work whose gates were locked on the inside with a horizontal bolt half way up. Some were easy; the bolts were fitted with a vertical wooden lever which came nearly level with the top of the gate. If not, you had to hang over and work the bolt upside down. Either way gates swung open suddenly. 'If they break their neck, who's liable?' the weathercock man asked. 'The occupier of the premises? Where's the justice of that?'

The adults would go for days without complaint then suddenly all the bedroom windows of the row would be flung open in erratic succession, each framing a deranged inmate. When young men came to play, the adults merely peered over yard gates and chunnered, though the noises then were heavier. The ball flew. It thudded against the sleeper fence, scuttered on the cinders, hit the walls with a resilient singing note and bobbled on the roof slates. Accustomed to the racket of the cotton mills, the inmates could bear the continuous shrieking of children better than these distinct sounds. It drove them to underhand tactics. They went and told my mother I had been over the fence on to the railway embankment. This was true. The young

men helped me over when we went to retrieve the ball and
we walked back through the long bleached grass of the
cutting to the bridge. This, I now learned, was at the very
top of the league table of sins, an offence so grievous that
prohibitions against it wrought in cast iron were displayed
at intervals along the track. It would not only displease
Jesus, it might well incur a fine of forty shillings.

My father was told. He cleaned the ball, inserted a new
leather lace and re-inflated it. He then massaged it with
dubbin and put it into a high cupboard to allow time for the
dubbin to sink in. I was alarmed; plant bulbs and tins of
biscuits which went into the cupboard were not seen again
for a long time. Real footballers, my father explained, were
in the same boat at this time of the year. They had to knock
off for four months. That was how cricket came to be
played. The only football played in summer was by children
too young to know better with rubber balls. The real leather
balls were all laid up absorbing their feed of dubbin. It
was clearly an immutable law of the universe, beyond
disputation. I asked for clogs to give me an equal chance
when the game resumed. He promised me a pair of heavy
boots. Summer arrived, dandelions flowered at the foot of
the fence of sleepers, peace returned.

My cousin Stanley Sephton Kerry showed early the begin-
nings of the qualities of his mature years: intelligence,
generosity, gentleness and quick humour. At the age of four
he was already different from any of the boys I played with.
He was an indoor boy. He did things with crayons and
paint and plasticine. He did not stick transfers on the back
of his hand but arranged the pictures properly on the pages
of a book and without an excess of water. He could see
properly only out of one eye. The poor one was said to be a
lazy eye so they equipped him with spectacles and covered
up the good one. He stumbled about until it was accepted
that the lazy eye was almost sightless, then he was fitted
with another pair of spectacles and had no more trouble
until he joined the army and had to get a dispensation to
aim with his good left eye. He could not judge speeds and
distances well enough to catch a ball. He never played

games. He belonged to no gangs. He did not shout. He had a contented and enclosed life to which he courteously admitted visitors. You could look at his books and his works. He was so generous in giving away things that auntie Abbie frisked visitors on their way out.

They lived on the same main road as us but in Britannia, half a mile back towards Bacup. When our families left the council estate they had found houses within walking distance of each other and the grandparents Sephton had taken up abode halfway between the two. Families usually wished to stick together and the large number of houses to let made it possible. Where the Kerrys lived the moors fell back from the road so their house at the end of a terrace overlooked meadows. A little further down the road on the opposite side were new brick houses of business and professional people. It pleased auntie Abbie that Stanley moved in these circles. The children she called his 'little playmates'.

His interests were open to anybody. He encouraged me to read, he taught me how to tell the time on a cardboard clock and how to make patterns with some sea shells he kept in a bucket in the yard. Although only four months older he seemed immensely knowledgeable. We were different in manner and in physique; he was big like auntie Abbie and dark like uncle Ben. When we were slightly older we took pleasure in being likened to Laurel and Hardy. We came to understand unspoken thoughts. We laughed together at jokes that had not been voiced. The first time I can remember feeling apprehension for somebody else was when they took him to the clinic with his eye. They said he was going to have drops in and he was going to be a brave boy. Grandma Sephton had the sofa ready for him when he came home, a ritual preparation for any ailment, but he caught sight in a mirror of the covered eye and made everybody laugh by peeping over the table and round the doors.

On weekdays at Stanley's house there was a sense of liberty because auntie Abbie had gone back to work in the slipper works and we were in the care of grandma Sephton who made up games for our amusement. We went through a period in which all the snacks between meals were stolen.

She would place what she had prepared on a table and say, 'Now I think that will be safe there, don't you?'

'Yes,' we answered, laughing at her gullibility.

'It won't disappear if I turn my back?'

'No.'

'The mice won't get it?'

'No,' we would chortle. 'Ho, ho, ho.'

She went out. We spluttered, choking with giggles, through the dripping toast and beef-tea. She was amazed to find nothing but crumbs. 'The mice,' we would shout, 'the mice'. Or sometimes we would confess, 'Disappeared down the red lane' and run for our lives.

On warm days she took us into the meadow for a picnic. When it was wet she settled us down to one of Stanley's pursuits or let us help her with toy brooms and carpet sweepers. Having been a domestic servant from the age of 12 until marriage she could work without annoyance while others scurried about. The presence of children was a pleasure rather than a distraction. She drew us into the work of preparing the dinner she made for uncle Ben and auntie Abbie, letting us put the fruit in pies and showing us how to set the table.

We explored the darkness of the cellar. It took days of creeping advance and headlong retreats to descend the stairs and penetrate across the floor to the outer door. We tugged it open. Daylight exploded into the cellar. The walls were not black but white. Mrs Fruin's washing equipment stood like hibernating creatures caught in sleep, the tub and posser, the washboard, the boiler with its tail of red rubber piping. Monday was the usual washing day but Mrs Fruin as a professional washed every day of the week and came to Kerrys' on Friday. I suppose it did not seem anachronistic then for auntie Abbie to employ a washerwoman even though they themselves could no longer afford a council rent and she was obliged to leave her young children and go out to work. At home we had a school-leaver, Irene Hopwood, who was employed several days of the week to help with Eric and wheel him out. The professional houses near Kerrys', in truth little bungalows, all had cleaning women and some had full-time domestic servants in white cuffs and lace collars. There seem to have been a lot of part-time jobs going even at working-class houses. They disappeared, I suppose, in the 1930s when there were no margins. After the war electrical gadgets did more of the work and domestic employment became a no-go area. Those who might have done it preferred any other job or none to working round somebody else's house, those who might have employed them begrudged any expenditure on service and preferred to mortgage their own leisure to do-it-yourself jobs. I think perhaps that in the 'twenties sharing was instinctive; it became a precept when the instinct died.

We discovered another way into the cellar, an iron trap door let into the public pavement in front of the house by which coal was delivered. We opened the trap, slid down the brick chute on to the coal, out through the cellar door, round the house and back down the chute. Stanley's little playmates arrived and joined the circuit. When apprehended we looked like dwarf colliers. A couple of crones protested at the front door about the danger to the public of the open trap, which caught uncle Ben on a tender spot because he was already faced with an action for damages by Mrs Fruin who had fallen down the cellar steps and broken her arm. An old woman down the coal chute would just about have cooked his goose. He remonstrated, conjuring up a vivid picture of himself ruined and behind bars that delighted us.

We turned our attention to another corner of the cellar. A glass cubicle like a telephone kiosk formed a lavatory in which a deep shaft dropped directly to the sewer. We filled it with sods. It must not have been in regular use because the job took us several days and was spotted only when grass peeped over the lavatory seat. Uncle Ben spent a retching Saturday afternoon unblocking the shaft. He took against me. Pranks in review became crimes. I had instigated the theft from the bread bin of loaves which we were caught gnawing on the outside steps. I had got up an expedition of Stanley's little playmates on tricycles and pedal cars aimed at Bacup centre. I had tricycled over a woman's foot. I had tried to drown a boy in a pit trap.

In truth it was another boy who had tricycled over the woman's foot, as grandma Sephton was at pains to point out, and the trap had proceeded from Stanley's scholarly researches. It was intended to catch a gorilla or a tiger. Following the printed plan which he pinned on the cellar door we dug a pit in the strip of back yard garden, filled it with water carried from the cellar in jam jars and scattered some blades of grass on the surface to conceal the trap from the victim's eye. No victim arrived. We admitted we had never had any real hope of a tiger or a gorilla but Stanley thought if we were patient we might still bag a passing tramp. None came. We found Miles Warmsley in the back street and offered him a stroll on our new lawn. He said the grass wasn't growing, it was floating on a pool. We denied it. There was a certain amount of arguing and hustling. His feet went in. Three days later his grandfather came round to report him down with a cold. He was being dosed, as we saw, with Fennings Fever Cure, an astringent nostrum that drew in his cheeks to the shape of a skull. The doctor was sent for. Pneumonia seemed likely to set in. Uncle Ben informed my mother in terms of great foreboding. Further clauses were added to my evening prayers: repentance, a request for the sparing and restoration of Miles Warmsley and an undertaking to refrain from further devising, digging, building or otherwise constructing man traps.

I was then spotted jogging along the tram tracks. A ball had lodged in one of the lines and started to roll with the gentle gradient of the road. I trotted after it and when at last I caught it I noticed a tram coming gently to rest behind me. I thought the driver and the passengers seemed amused. But uncle Ben was among them and he had a very different account. I should make it clear that although he kept me taped he was a benign man, moderate in judgment and without malice. However, perhaps because of Irish in his ancestry, he was incapable of telling any story without wild exaggeration. Passengers, he told my mother, watched aghast, the driver stamped on the brake with teeth clenched and eyes closed, the tracks glowed red under locked screeching wheels, the trolley crackled with purple light, pedestrians fainted. All adults lived in fantasy. My mother took uncle Ben's work of art and reprocessed it for her own. Miles

Warmsley was dropped from the prayer and his place taken by sentiments related to tramways. The cognate matter of trespass on the railway was revived and included where the text permitted.

3 · GRANDFATHER SEPHTON

When Stanley started school my grandfather Sephton took to calling for me. I gathered he had been engaged as a substitute playmate. He proved more than satisfactory. He was at this time, 1928, sixty-one years old, small and spruce with a moustache and a fine silver quiff. He had something of the air of a marshal of France. He spoke to everyone, though without the familiarities of address which were normal in the district, and everyone responded from children in push chairs to dripping old men. He was especially good at drawing out bashful youths and maidens as he called them. Life was drama; he gloried in his own role and encouraged others in the performance of theirs. It was also celebration, the double pleasure of events enjoyed as they happened and savoured at the retelling. Something was always happening.

I went with him collecting premiums for the Refuge Assurance company. On two mornings a week we followed tracks that climbed over the horizon of the moors to farmsteads in patchworks of fields kept green by constant manure-spreading. Some had a small lake and a shelter belt of trees; the only other trees on the moors were clumps of hawthorn. The houses were dark and floored with flagstones that resonated as though deep cellars lay below. The farm women were fatter than those we lived amongst who worked in the mills and if the man was up on the moor they would call him from the door in a voice that made the pots rattle. One woman who was ironing and nodding to an inaudible rhythm lifted from her head a fitting I had not

seen before and placed it on mine. I was terrified to hear
loud music.

The sky was always one rise beyond where we went and
though we tried we never reached it. Either time pressed or
it was raining. One day in spring we found the spread of
the moors ahead of us burning, fired to improve the new
grass. The breeze carried the bark of dogs excited by the
flames and the bleat of sheep gathered for safety into the
folds. Smoke billowed across the horizon. In places we
passed close to the fires. The blackened earth smouldered
and from its edges a glowing tide spread outward, snatched
at a clump of old grass and straddled flame across ten or
twenty yards. When the wind changed, men ran about in
the smoke slogging at the fire with their jackets to keep it
from the buildings. A bachelor who lived alone had gone
down to the valley with the milk and come back and found
his house burned down. The air was loud with birds whose
nests the fire destroyed.

One summer morning we stopped on the moors and
listened to the school which lay below us by the road, a
new building surrounded by lawns and paths. Voices recited
a multiplication table, then other voices the different rhythm
of a verse, then a piano sounded and the voices sang. We

heard other sounds, birds, the hum of cotton mills, the clanking and coughing of the railway, a motor vehicle passing small in the road. The school sound was dominant although no one was to be seen but a solitary boy who closed a door behind him and crossed the yard.

My grandmother had our dinner ready, and she herself waited eagerly to hear of our encounters. Her role, which greatly pleased her, was to react with astonishment. She would look in bright-eyed amazement from one to the other of us, conferring on us a partnership to which she stood slightly outside. 'Well, I never did!' she would exclaim. In some of his stories I was actually able to recognise some event of the morning. 'Well, I never. That is a caution.'

She cleared the table, spread the prickly plush cloth over it, then they cashed up, making piles of the coins he had collected and muttering in unison as they followed together the columns of figures in the ledger. Neither was good at arithmetic. It took a long time and was not always resolved. The billiard table called. He would rise and say gently 'It's close enough, my love'. She looked alarmed. He laid a hand on her head. 'It's quite in order.' We then took the tram to the Liberal club. It was not quite in order, as events were soon to prove, but any lingering anxieties he might have had fled as he cracked the balls up and down the table. I was allowed to make shots using the scoreboard stick as a cue and left to practice while he played whist with ancient men.

We went to the market and hot gospel meetings and the library reading room. We went to the pictures where people admonished each other with planks and a brisk lady at the piano bounded along in time with Rin-tin-tin. My grandfather seemed to know everybody in Bacup. All kinds of people came to us with tales. Young men sometimes removed their cap. In April we went up through the sombre streets to Lane Head cricket ground where at the opening of the heavy gate the world broke into colour, green field, white sightscreens, red pavilion, a chestnut horse pulling a mowing machine with the groundsman perched on his iron saddle and a spume of grass rising in their wake. It was an excitement also of smells: the mown grass, whitewash which men on ladders applied to the perimeter walls and splashed liberally across the cinders of the track, linseed oil and embrocation in the pavilion where the floorboards were stippled with the spikes of cricket boots, beery urine at the corrugated lavatories, the mellow aroma of years of tea and Oxo at the hut which my grandfather, unable to change the habit of his early years, persisted in calling the refreshment tent. Sometimes the players practiced at the nets and when we were very lucky we would see the new Australian professional Arthur J. Richardson, a correct and stylish cricketer whom my grandfather greatly admired.

Once on our return journey from town the tram was derailed by a workman's pick left on the line. The trolley, dislodged from its cable, swung above our heads on the open upper deck. 'We must say nothing,' he said. 'It might alarm your grandmother.' But of course he did: how quick we ducked, how narrowly we had escaped decapitation or at least injury to his bowler hat, our climb out down stairs nearly horizontal, the passengers below in a heap against the windows. 'Well, I never did,' she said. 'That is a caution!' I have a clear memory of this near-fatal accident and another one, no less clear, of a tram disappointingly upright with its front wheels standing a couple of inches out of the track.

Telling her his stories was a greater pleasure than the events. It was as though nothing had really happened until he told her about it. I started to tell stories to my mother who, having a good sense of humour, gave them an extra twist which lifted them into the realm of the ludicrous. Our laughter set off my brother Eric, and his laughter in turn increased ours because he had no idea what we were laughing at. The stories created a bond, a rejoicing in exaggeration, which was the stronger between us because my father did not understand it and did not quite like it. As the years went by it peopled our locality with clowns.

I watched cricket matches less often with my grandfather than with my mother and grandmother. They and my mother's two sisters had been among the first women to watch Lancashire League matches. They had always gone to cricket in the country and when they arrived in Bacup in 1911 they turned up at Lane Head as a matter of Saturday

afternoon habit. The crowd shocked them. It looked and
behaved like a football crowd, spitting, swearing and barracking the players. Their presence in turn shocked the
crowd. It was known that women were beginning to behave
in outrageous ways, painting their faces, demanding the
vote and driving motor cars. But not in Bacup. Unaware
perhaps of the degree of consternation they caused, my
grandmother and her daughters persisted in going to Lane
Head and compounded the offence by travelling to away
matches. Other women followed their example. Thus a trail
was blazed or the rot set in, however you care to look at it.

There was a practical objection to women, which was
that they spoiled men's enjoyment. From the growling
barrage of barracking which rumbled through the afternoon
single shots cracked out from time to time which so visibly
hit a target that the whole ground laughed. Few could do it
well. It required a powerful voice, brevity, a robust sense
of humour, and timing. Some afternoons the competition
between the barrackers took on such life that the match
itself dwindled to a charade played by white ghosts. Quite a
few of the wits who could reach the opposite boundary
with their vocal sallies turned out on acquaintance to be
weedy little men, residents, it was generally believed, of
female-dominated homes, who had developed their talent
on the only afternoon when they were free to open their
mouths. There was a second recreation in the crowd, argu-
ments which growled on all afternoon. They arose from
what happened on the field but ranged into the history and
laws of the game. Occasionally an argument would flare out
from the group where it began and spread round the
boundary until it was peremptorily confined. 'Thou'rt not
sitting on this form. Shut thi mouth.' Scorn and ridicule
were the main weapons. Crude wit was used like a club.
This again was not a pastime to be comfortably enjoyed in
the presence of ladies. The matter was eventually resolved
by a policy of apartheid. The lower ground, where admission
was cheaper and the forms had no backrests, remained the
preserve of men. Women went on the pavilion side where
they obligingly affected to be out of earshot. Men who

insisted on bringing their ladies were expected to accept banishment with them to the higher ground.

My grandfather spared himself this penance. He saw us through our turnstile and then repaired to his own. We would spot his bowler hat among the cloth caps at the opposite boundary as he eased himself in and started an argument. He was a dancing master among pugilists, a swordsman among the knobkerries. He assumed a fine rhetorical style, having modelled himself on Mr Gladstone who modelled himself on Socrates. He knew how to engage support by courteous acknowledgment of those keen to get into the discussion and he would attempt by patient questioning to draw his antagonist into an assertion that could be disproved by the printed record. He would then draw out his Wisden's Guide to the Lancashire League which he knew by heart, and from across the ground we would see him passing it up, opened at the appropriate page, to the jury of faces behind him.

One Saturday Leary Constantine arrived. He was the professional with Nelson Cricket Club, the first West Indian to play in the Lancashire League, and the first black man I saw. The whole crowd rose in a buzz of excitement when he appeared striding down the pavilion steps. Constantine was an instinctive player, sharp-eyed and agile. He moved his feet and opened his shoulders and belted and punched the ball with an abandon nobody had seen before. When he had rattled up a good score he performed antics. He would play balls through his legs, go down the wicket and volley them, hook off-breaks and run desperate singles. He was soon among the records in my grandfather's Wisden. Everybody loved him. My grandfather admired the man but disliked his style and influence. Buffoonery apart, it was not cricket to play shots into the air and to bowl at a pace so uncontrolled in bad overs that he gave away a dozen byes and menaced the windows in Greensnook Lane.

Constantine's display accentuated an argument in which my grandfather had been at odds with those who sat around him. They were nearly all by choice football spectators. Cricket served to pass the idle months between one football season and the next. They wanted it played fast and violently

and they scorned the orthodox style of the Bacup professional Arthur Richardson. A man said Richardson had
one boot repaired at a time. My grandfather said if it was
his right boot it was reasonable; he dragged the toe at the
bowling crease. The man said he wasn't talking about his
cricket boots but his ordinary footwear. In that case, my
grandfather said, it was irrelevant. They thought not; they
perceived a meanness of spirit that was reflected in his
cautious style of batting. In the end a man who had barely
spoken came to my grandfather's assistance with an argument deplorably irrelevant and deplorably effective. Australians, he said, we had come to accept, but did we really have
any need for niggers to come here to teach us to play cricket?

When winter came we went to the adjoining ground to
watch Bacup football team play in the Lancashire Combi-
nation. The players in black and amber stripes looked like a
pack of men who had been hired to play tigers but forgotten
the heads. The game looked what it was, a by-product of
heavy industry. Many of the players were coal miners; on
wet days they needed the stamina. The field was a swamp,
the leather ball heavy with absorbed water, their long shorts
and woollen socks sodden. Play when it came to the near
touchline moved at frightening speed. I pitied the players
for the pain of their efforts that narrowed their eyes and
made them gasp. They were often floored but seldom stayed
down. Besides me on a bench in front of the wooden stand
sat the trainer. He sat alone. The gangs of anguished men in
track suits snarling through chewing gum were a refinement
only the distant future would enjoy. The trainer was in sole
charge and what he was in charge of was the sponge. It
floated in a bucket of icy water which in moments of high
excitement he tapped with his foot. When a player went
down he rose and loped across the mud, making arcs of
water droplets from the sponge swung in his hand. He
applied it to the back of the neck. The player's limbs would
jerk as though an electric current had been put through him,
then he would be on his feet not knowing where he was but
eagerly nodding, all right, fine, thanks, backing off from
further treatment. If a player persisted in unconsciousness

the trainer doubled him up, lifted his collar wide and wrung out the sponge on his spine. It was known as the magic sponge, and justifiably. Men knocked dateless often revived completely before the sponge even reached them.

One Saturday before the match my grandfather allowed me to join some boys who were kicking a ball round one of the penalty areas. It was a leather ball but stuffed with paper. The number of players varied from minute to minute. Thirty or forty would scuffle round then groups would break away and leave, passing new players as they arrived across the pitch. It looked like a changeover in American football performed by stunted scarecrows. Nobody observed any rules. There were anything up to a dozen dwarf goal-keepers under the crossbar. Players shoved each other or tackled rugby fashion. I had hoped to play an outstanding game to impress my grandfather who stood behind the goal and perhaps even catch the eye of the trainer as he emerged from the stand with his bucket. Unable to get near, I adopted the unorthodox tactics of the other players. I knocked one boy down, threw another with a neck-hold and got in a first kick at the ball. It was my last. My grandfather marched me off. 'That's not the game at all, son!' He was outraged. In a single moment I had violated the spirit of sportsmanship, public propriety and the rule of law. It was the only time I ever knew him angry with me, a bad debut in what I had begun to cherish as my future profession.

Lancashire was still then the main centre of League football and one Saturday we went to the great event of the year, the First Division match between Burnley and Blackburn Rovers. It was evident from the moment we got off the tram in Bacup centre that something momentous was gathering. Along the pavement where I had never seen more than two of the green Todmorden corporation motor buses standing there were now half a dozen and men were crossing the road towards them with a gleeful haste never seen on weekdays. Whatever identities dulled their days, weaver, collier, husband, shopkeeper or circuit steward, they now sloughed off. They were football spectators. They wore a uniform of tweed overcoats and cloth caps, smoked pipes which transformed the bus into a mobile gas chamber and

waited bright-eyed for a chance to join in the rumble of
argument and opinion. I felt sorry for the telegraph poles as
they flitted past and fell behind because they would spend
their whole life standing on the moor and never be part of a
football crowd.

Outside the ground my grandfather guided me, hands on
shoulders, into the press and darkness of a queue. I could
hear the programme sellers and the clatter of police horses
and, as we approached, the clicking of many turnstiles, but
I could see only in glimpses beyond the prickling hair of the
overcoats that buffed me from all sides. I saw above us the
great brick cliff of the back of the main stand, then my
grandfather spoke into a turnstile and the keeper whom I
could not see said 'Lift him over'. I was hoisted above his
rotating gate into the darkness under the rumbling boards of
the stand. Beyond in the daylight of the pitch a brass band
was marching.

We were not known at Burnley and my grandfather had
to negotiate a seat for me on the bench by the trainer. The
bench ran for thirty or forty yards. Others who were
privileged to use it, I noticed, were not small boys but men
with one leg who hoisted themselves down and stored their
crutches under the seat. Beyond them the whole length of
the wall filled up with invalid carriages, some pushed, most
hand-propelled by cripples who churned handles or heaved
the wheels round directly with the heels of their thumbs.
Most of these men were casualties of the war. The sight of
them was as unremarkable in those years as the sight of
colliers with black faces and weavers white with cotton
down. Few of those on crutches wore overcoats because, I
suppose, of the cost and the difficulty of getting in and out
of them. Their jackets were patched with leather at places
the crutches wore. They must often have been cold.

Pennies fell in a shower, spangles on the cinder track and
the grass in front of me. Four men were approaching along
the touchline holding a sheet already weighted down by
coins. One looking up towards the stand mouthed an appeal,
'Support the band, please'. Another nodded and sawed
thanks with his free hand like a mechanical doll. Youths
assisting them scrabbled in the grass and cinders for thrown

pennies that missed the sheet. I was caught by surprise by a great roar that knocked me back as though the sea had come on top of me and reduced the band to silent mime. The teams were coming out. It was as though the stand and terraces were drawn upwards and inwards by the volume of their own noise, great banks of faces like a massive display of ping-pong balls on the terraces, greyer in the shade of the stand behind the goal and lost at the back in darkness where matches struck like darting fireflies. The contour of the pitch added to the claustration, slightly raised along the middle, so that down on my bench I was level with the players' boots. Those on my side thundered past like giants, those on the other wing were almost lost beyond the horizon. The clamour of the crowd resolved itself into different moods, crowing, jeering, exhorting, booing, protesting, all with a passion that threatened to crack the walls of faces and bring them cascading down on to the pitch. Dazed with the noise and mesmerised by the speed of play, I could get no grasp of the game. Incidents happened in rapid succession, each of desperate importance and each immediately effaced by the next. Then they were trooping off. How long had they been playing? It seemed less than five minutes. My grandfather spoke; his voice was resonant and distant as it sounded back at home when I was only half awake. The band, audible again, came marching round.

The second half was longer and more coherent. The trainer had more to do and the familiarity close beside me of the business with the sponge and bucket lessened the feeling of having been dropped to the bottom of a huge foreign well. Then it was over. The walls of menacing faces crumbled and disintegrated, and from the gates, apologising to those they jostled, making way for the old and the lame, came a crowd of mild and jocular men like those who had come with us on the bus. They walked down Brunshaw road, filling its whole width, the ritual ended, the week fulfilled, thousands of heads and shoulders flowing past under the gas lights.

Nearly all the houses in Troughgate and Britannia were strung along Rochdale road, but there were a number of unpaved side streets that ended at hen pens or petered out

into farm tracks. My grandparents lived in a house at the gable end of one of these rows overlooking the main road. It was elevated three steps above the pavement, and the window of the living room was a good spot to watch the motors from. One day my grandmother set me to watch for the gingerbread boy. I could not believe such a boy existed yet she never told tall stories. Was he really a gingerbread boy? I asked. Yes, he was. Then how would he come along the road? Pedalling his bike as I would see directly. Did he have currants for his eyes and buttons? Be off with your bother. She had no imagination, no inkling of the notion that caused my wonder. He stopped at the door and opened the delivery box of his tricycle, a boy in a floppy cloth cap, the disappointing victim of a transferred epithet. 'There now,' she said, opening the bag of biscuits for me, 'are you satisfied?'

On Fridays we 'went down the mine'. The fire was left unlighted and she shovelled up ash from a pit beneath it about three feet deep. Where it hardened in corners she prodded with a poker and chased the last deposits with her shovel scraping and squeaking against the sides of the pit. The ash, dancing in the shafts of light from the window, tickled our noses and we had to take care when we sneezed to turn away from the big bucket into which she was shovelling. We carried the bucket up the side street to an ash tip which smelt of sodden tea leaves and burnt things but was brightened with salmon and pineapple tins from Sunday tea times. We black-leaded the grate and brushed the square of carpet, having first scattered wet tea leaves on it to prevent dust from rising. We dusted round, polished the furniture and finally watered all the plants, taking care not to give too much to the one that hung in a wire basket behind the front door lest some visitor got a shower bath. Every morning the chamber pots were emptied into a white enamel slop bucket, fitted for decency with a lid, which was carried to the shared water closet by the ash tip. It was the custom to pretend not to notice anyone engaged on this errand. Two women who plonked their buckets down and stopped for a conversation were felt to be unsuited to the neighbourhood.

On Friday afternoons we bought the groceries at the Co-op which was across the side street. Half a dozen assistants in tasselled aprons bobbed about in front of a bank of wooden drawers, weighing out sugar and flour and currants and raisins, slapping butter, cutting cheese with a wire and bacon with a knife worn with sharpening to an arc like a scimitar. They made rapid bags of different shapes and sizes, square for the bigger quantities, conical for small measures such as coconut and cream of tartar and the red Cayenne pods which added fire to my grandparents' morning tea. Nothing was packaged. Everything was open to sight and to flies whose number in summer time seemed undiminished by the lost legions stuck on the gently twirling strips of fly paper above the counter. There was sawdust on the floor and the air was fragrant with the smell of fruit and ham and biscuits.

We were in there a long time. The shop was always full on pay day mainly of older women in shawls. They took their time, ordering each item separately and waiting until the assistant had brought it back and bagged it up before beginning to consider the next. They used the intervals to hold conversations or start badinage which might spark

along the line of assistants and backfire through the customers. Some ladies were too old to join in the jokes and a
few too dateless to know quite what they wanted. They
would be ushered forward before their turn and the customers and shopmen would prompt them with suggestions.
Sometimes the ordering was taken out of an old woman's
hands completely. There would be a general debate over her
head about what she needed, what she might like but
shouldn't have, who might be visiting her, what they might
fancy for their tea and what on the other hand was known
to bring them out in a rash. Then there were dividend
cheques to be written on pads full of carbons with a copying
ink pencil which the assistants kept behind their ears and
used at the end of the purchase to tap each of the bags in
totting up the total. When we came out of the Co-op the
day had moved on. Sometimes the children were running
home from school.

My grandmother bought some of her groceries from
James Duckworth's across the road and sometimes we visited
the sub-post office and general store of Jonas Horsfall. He
was a bald, lugubrious man who had personally witnessed
the motor accident that downed Peter Pilling. I thought his
mournfulness had been occasioned by the happening but
when it persisted after Peter's recovery I decided it must
be because he had lost his hair. His unctuousness was a
characteristic of shopkeepers, not of the secure employees of
the Co-op whose familiarity could verge on the impertinent,
but of small shopkeepers who had to grovel to stay in
business. His pandering combined the gratuitous chastisement of children with an apparent disregard for the promotion of his own trade. 'Make 'em last,' a woman would
say, handing a child a bag of his sweets. 'They bolt 'em
down and then they're sick,' Jonas Horsfall echoed. 'They
don't think on.' My grandfather bought me a hard red
cricket ball. He offered the observation that I could never
learn to bowl with a ball without a seam, a technical sort of
bouncer which flew well over Mr Horsfall's pate. 'And
when they get 'em,' he lamented, ringing up the money,
'they only knock 'em through people's windows.' It was

the wrong thing to say. My grandfather did not demur but he did not assent. Poor Mr Horsfall looked pained, caught in the trap of saying something silly which he did not particularly believe.

4 · BRITANNIA SCHOOL

At home the main object of interest was my brother Eric, now in his second year, who made us laugh by mimicking the actions of human beings. Anything that moved held his wide-eyed attention. Suspended by elastic over his pram was a Dismal Desmond, a squatting spotted dog, which swung and bounced when you tugged. It kept him occupied for hours. I had a large tin top that could be pumped to speed by a handle with a spiral thread and would then spin on the oilcloth and hum a wordless song that Eric joined in. A boy who came to the house said 'Cat's chorus' and when the top spun after that my mother and I laughed at the recollection of the remark and my brother at our laughter and we again because he did not know what he was laughing at. Music charmed his spirit. He would bang his spoon for repeated performances of our only record on my tin gramophone. On one side somebody croaked the hymn:

Son of my soul, thou Saviour dear
It is not night if Thou art near.

On the other side a more frivolous vocalist sang:

I'm knee deep in daisies
I'm head over heels in love.

Both sides of the record got scratched and we had the pleasure of hearing the singers stuck in the groove bleating out the same sounds again and again like hens locked into a hut at sunset.

There were other things to improve the mind: big wooden jigsaws, one with a picture of a donkey, the other of a bear, and the building blocks which I was taught to regard not as missiles but as an aid to literacy. Each had a letter of the alphabet on it and a picture of an animal of a species that began with that letter. Some such as Q for quagga were difficult to remember because unlike H for horse or C for cow they could not be readily pointed out in Troughgate. In fact I never came across a quagga and, turning at last to the dictionary, I see why. Even all those years ago it had already disappeared from the earth. 'Extinct,' the dictionary says, 'S. Afr. equine quadruped related to ass and zebra, less striped than latter (f. Xhosa-Kaffir iqwara)'. I was still struggling with the bricks while cousin Stanley was lolling on the sofa reading Dickens.

Britannia school was a new building which smelled of concrete and sawn wood. On my first day I was given a model farmyard to play with. It also was new. Most of the animals still had all their legs. The next day I was allowed only a short session with the farm and after that it was made clear that I was finished with agriculture and must begin to prepare for whatever role life might have in store.

I gave the impression of learning effortlessly. Put to sit by Stanley, I simply followed his voice in recitations, songs and class readings, and copied letters and figures from his exercise book. Eventually we had to read aloud solo and that unmasked me. I was a backward reader. I was so backward that I did not know the word and, believing it might be an accolade, went home and told my mother. She was grieved after all the work we had done together with the quaggas and my faultless rendering of my nightly prayers including variable clauses added at short notice. I had seemed to be well launched towards the ambition she and my grandmother had for me of becoming a cricketing parson like the character in the Sunday Companion after whom I had been named. I was proficient with the bat, I had bowled all the red paint off the hard ball bought at Jonas Horsfall's, but this would be a lopsided development of talent if I grew up unable to read the Good Book. She went to see the

teacher who wisely decided not to move me away from
Stanley but to shift me to his right where I could not so
easily see what he was writing. It was explained that I must
acquire an independent store of knowledge, otherwise I
would go through life depending on Stanley to read docu-
ments to me and show me where to put my mark.

Miss Cockcroft undertook a campaign to liquidate my
illiteracy. She stood behind me as the class read aloud,
pointing out the words with a long polished finger nail. She
had, like my mother, a kind face and a gentle voice and in
her close presence I felt the same comfort. The back of my
head rested against her thighs. I could smell her perfume
and hear her voice distinct in the chant of the class reading.
It was bliss. I made slow progress at reading.

Each morning my grandmother gave Stanley some lunch
to be shared between us and eaten at playtime. It was crisp
dripping toast. He did the sharing conscientiously, breaking
any odd extra piece in two under the desk. Miss Cockcroft
came to inspect the pile of crumbs. She made no fuss but it
emerged that the concept of lunch was foreign to her.
She proposed some synonyms which were foreign to us.
Children who had hitherto allowed us to gobble unmolested
gathered round in the playground now it was known that
what we were eating was lunch, which even the teacher did
not understand. The word is not used in East Lancashire
either for the mid-day meal, which is dinner, or as my
grandmother used it for a snack in mid-morning. Some
small children stalked round shouting the word and a bigger
boy sought to participate in the repast. For a round of toast
he would stick up for us. Who against? Against all them
that want to bash you. The offence was clear enough. We
had been caught out in a ritual as outlandish as beating
tom-tom drums or smoking Gauloises. Stanley refused to
surrender the toast. It was now invested with a mystical
quality in our eyes as well as theirs, not to be distributed
among the uncircumcised Philistines. But with a fine diplomatic sense he offered our protector a braid of Spanish to be
delivered in the afternoon. It was black shiny stuff coiled
round a small coloured sweet and looked when stretched
out like a leather belt. The boy went on his hands and knees

round the cloakroom with the Spanish dangling from his mouth and grunting like a pig. He said he would make us laugh again for any further confectionery put his way.

Many boys could pee over the wall of the lavatories. On a good day sparkling jets rose and fell the length of playtime. Size made no difference; some of the smallest and youngest boys were the best. The less able steamed and stank for their pains. My mother urged the view that greater honour was to be won at football and cricket. Among the organised games we played at school was one which I suppose could only be considered part of our war studies. Two lines of children faced each other across the playground. One would advance singing:

> We will set our dogs on you for we are the Romans.
> We will set our dogs on you, we are the Roman soldiers.

The other line would then prance to meet the challenge singing in reply:

> We don't care for your dogs or you, for we are the English.
> We don't care for your dogs or you, we are the English soldiers.

There would then be an exchange of imaginary missiles with sound effects. But neither the enemy nor the weaponry was clear. Some sang 'Romans' and some sang 'Germans'. Some hurled javelins, some fired arrows, and some mowed down the opposite half of the infants' class with traversing maching guns.

We all went home to dinner. In the afternoon we had a sleep, heads on the desk, which made our necks and cheek bones ache. At 3.30 we went with a higher class to the hall to sing 'Now the day is over' and say a prayer. My day ceased to end with Amen. I was kept in for misdemeanours. My mother waiting at the gate saw Stanley approach alone and was dismayed to learn that I was serving another sentence. For one offence I was sent to stand on the platform at the end of the hall with a hardened delinquent in oversized clogs. 'Don't sing,' he ordered me when Miss Cockcroft struck up the hymn at the piano, and when at the end I put my hands together for the prayer he knocked them down.

'We're not going home. Bugger 'em.' It was a precept I had been groping towards.

For my mother the eventual effect of these detentions was not to increase but to allay the concern she felt about my conduct. The teachers, Miss Cockcroft, and Miss Unwin from the higher class who took command in the hall, made nothing of the incidents. They were everyday misdemeanours which some children committed more often than others. Their unconcern surprised my mother. The puritanical tradition of her upbringing was insensitive to distinction between different degrees of waywardness. Any misconduct was cause for anxiety, judgment, repentance and prayer. At first she was rather shocked by the teachers' unconcern but then agreeably surprised that nobody was asking her or me to answer for anything. But why, she now asked herself, did she always think there was something to answer for? Who appointed the judges? On what ground did they judge? She began to perceive censoriousness as a game played for domination and to recognise for the first time what an incongruous figure her father had cut when he resorted to it as a means of bolstering up his authority over teenage daughters. She began to feel free of the invisible presence of the elders and from the anxiety which can be a permanent state under the eyes of the sanctimonious.

There were other liberating influences. She came to know more people separately from her family. She began to belong. The boisterous manners of the district which at first alarmed her now appealed to her sense of humour. She was the centre of the home and the object of love. At the age of thirty she finally escaped the identity of the youngest child of a late Victorian family and emerged confident, competent and independent.

Some afternoons she let me stay in the schoolyard kicking a ball with bigger boys. She waited at the railings with my brother in the pram in the company of other mothers. We often had toast for tea. She would carefully remove a coal and I would toast thick bread by the glow, enjoying the warmth and the sense of the day ended and the pictures in the caves of the fire. It was a good home and Troughgate was a good place. My parents who had gone there as an economy were sorry when the time came to move on.

5 · FORMER TIMES

For several weeks before we moved to Burnley we stayed for some reason of convenience with the grandparents Sephton. Sometimes on wet afternoons when the money and the intractable ledgers had been moved from the table my grandfather screwed a monocle into his eye and fell to repairing watches, a small neat man tip-tapping with the tiny tools of the trade. He had learned watch-making as a boy in his father's workshop. My grandmother said it was a thousand pities he had been compelled to give it up. I did not know why. I thought she regretted it as part of the loss of the vivid days of his childhood, the olden days, which teemed in his account with characters and incident.

His very entry to the world, it seemed, had been high drama, wrestling with death in the first moments of life. He was not expected to last the night. He was baptised with haste and christened Edwin, in hope, after a pagan king of Northumbria who, being persuaded to perceive the brevity of this life in the flight of a sparrow across his hall, enrolled for the longer option. My grandfather was the fourth in a family of twelve children who fed along a dresser; the youngest at the end grew up left-handed because his right arm was imprisoned against the wall. One event followed another. Their house went on fire, smoking into the public gaze a recluse miser who lived next door, their father was hobbled in a spectacular crash on a penny-farthing, their grandfather an old soldier was cast in gaol after an altercation with the town clerk on the town hall steps and released through popular clamour. Edwin himself, oppressed by a demonic headmaster, sank into the delirium of erysipelas, came to bald and was transferred to a Church school where the vicar attended on Tuesdays and Fridays and thrashed publicly all who mocked the new boy's pate. The instruction there struck deep. One afternoon my grandfather set aside the watches and recited for me from the Catechism which, as a Nonconformist, he had not spoken for more than fifty years. It brought to mind a story he had not hitherto told of two childhood friends who kept a caged canary which on a wicked impulse he could not even now explain he had released and allowed to escape through the open window and over the roof tops. I was aware of a guilty undertow of vague understanding. I heard the beat of the wall clock which he had earlier oiled and reset. He put his monocle back into his eye and returned to his watches.

I imagined his boyhood in bright colour like the pictures of a book, as unconfined in time and place as a fairy story. It was a surprise to discover that my mother knew some of the landmarks, and then to learn that auntie Abbie had once been a child and indeed that all the people I knew had once been different ages and had known each other before any knew me. The discovery that one is not the centre of the universe, the focal point of all relationships, is difficult at first to comprehend, but I did begin to see similarities which I did not share between one and another of my relatives and in particular between photographs of my cousin Evelyn and my mother as a child. They were in fact related only through marriage and not alike but in facing the camera each had held her head and narrowed her eyes in the same way against the photographer's lights; and because of this resemblance I had, when my mother's childhood was spoken of, the image of a real person and a more sober expectation of events.

She was born in 1898 at Whiston, now a place name in the desolation of Merseyside but then a country village with a single coal pit separated by six miles of farmers' fields from the city of Liverpool. She was christened Alice. She had two older sisters, Abigail and Evaline, and many cousins in the family of pit workers to which her mother belonged. The girls were brought up in a style they were taught to consider bounteous. Their rented cottage stood alone in its garden. They kept a dog and a pig and rabbits. They had three meals a day and sometimes, if a visiting preacher came to dinner, a roast on Sunday. Before each meal they asked a blessing. Ingratitude for food was not tolerated. Anything left reappeared at the next meal. On working days their father had his meals alone at the end of his walk home from the watch factory at Prescot three miles away. Any delicacy was saved for him. He got a whole egg to himself. While he ate, the children were turned out of the room.

They were not forbidding parents. Theirs was perhaps the first generation of working people sufficiently well off to enjoy their children rather than to regard them as drones to be put to work as soon as they could stand. Decorative clothing was now to be bought for children. In a photograph taken outside the front door of their cottage in 1903 the girls wear print dresses with wide skirts. Two have bows in their hair and one wears a necklace. Across the dusty lane a tot of two or three watches from under the shade of a bonnet nearly as large as herself. In winter they were all heavily clothed. Houses were damp and draughty and heated only by a single fire. The Sephtons locked all their windows against the night air and arranged clothes maidens draped with blankets round the children's beds. Night in the sad story books was the time of death. Before they went to bed they prayed at their mother's knee:

> Lord, keep us safe this night,
> Secure from all our fears.
> May angels guard us while we sleep
> Till morning light appears.

They tried to start musical soirées. They got an organ with creaking pedals. Abigail was given expert tuition and was expected in turn to teach the two younger girls. As the first child she was treated as though she was much older than the others. It was she who fed the pig and lifted big stones in the garden and brought the evening paper from the village after dark in winter. She was serious and purposeful, and exasperated both by her own incompetence at the organ and the frivolity of her pupils. The attempt at a hymn

singing evening was disastrous. Abigail could not play, their
mother could not sing, the two younger girls were voiceless
with suppressed laughter and their father like many little
men prized his powerful and resonant voice and sang in his
own time. In chapel he imposed his tempo on organ, choir
and congregation. In the parlour it was more than Abigail
could manage to work the pedals, stops and keyboard
without his competition. It ended in tears. When she married, the organ was given to Abigail. She kept it in a dark
corner like a dangerous dog.

The prosperous years ended with a bewildering shock.
The watch factory closed. Moreover there was nowhere else
in Britain where watches were still made. It was inexplicable.
British industries in those days were not expected to collapse.
The workers at Prescot raised an emigration fund and saw
off to the United States the first of their workmates who
would spy out the promised land on behalf of the rest. They
never met again. The fund ran out. Those left behind never
worked again at their trade.

My grandfather was then 40. He worked through the
summer as a gardener for the vicar and the squire, then at
the onset of winter descended, a slight and delicate man,
into labouring jobs of the sort that made the cruel comedy
of early films. He joined the endless chain of men at the
cable works who marched to the point of collapse carrying
reels over their shoulder between factory and warehouse,
then inquiring for lighter work he was fixed up in all
innocence by his wife's cousins at Whiston pit with a job as
a blacksmith's striker. He was still reverberating when the
family migrated to East Lancashire in search of work.

To people from outside, the cotton towns must have been
overpowering in the boom of those Edwardian days. Bacup
at 850 feet was at the end of the railway line up the
Rossendale valley, a cluster of mill chimneys in a horseshoe
of the moors. Smoke blotted out the sun. There was a shop
on every corner, a pub in every street, chapels and chip
shops everywhere. The mill towns bustled with the business
of producing cotton for the world. The working week lasted
56 hours.

My mother and her sisters found jobs at the slipper works. They started at six and broke at eight for half an hour for breakfast. On her first day Alice at 13 lost all sense of time. When the second break came and the machines stopped again she was dismayed to learn it was only dinner time, not the end of the day. The afternoon, the week and the years stretched ahead. The First World War broke out to the universal acclamation of factory workers. Wherever the photographs were taken, London or Manchester, Munich or Paris, the faces in the crowds are the same, rapturous at liberation from the endless hum and clatter of machinery and from working days that for half the year began before daybreak and ended after nightfall.

Alice was luckier than most. Her success in a school-leaving examination came to light and she was promoted within weeks to a job in the store room at the top of the building, sorting on to shelves empty shoe boxes which were delivered by means of an outside hoist. They were winched up from ground level in a net and she would lean out of a doorway high in the wall and grab a stay rope as it swung past. The job was risky. She had feared heights from early childhood when she had a recurrent dream of falling in a slow glide down the steps of Whiston chapel into darkness where the devil waited. And here sharing the top floor of the factory was a powerful mephistophelian man, the manager, quartered in a glass cubicle from which frightened people scurried with his commands to all parts of the factory. The workmen on the ground shouted encouragement and occasionally hoisted up a chocolate or a cake with the load. Familiarity lulled her fears. On her fourteenth birthday she bearded the manager in his cubicle and asked if she should not have a rise. His laughter shook the shelves of shoe boxes. He gave her a rise.

There was a job of some sort for everybody in Bacup in 1911. Alice's father was taken on by the Refuge Assurance company and her grandfather past paid employment, was made superintendent of the Sunday school. A suitor arrived for Abigail, Benjamin Kerry, a cabinet maker she had thought to have left behind at his bench in St Helens. He presented himself boldly in the broad light of day riding a brand-new bicycle and dressed like a nigger minstrel. He had got a job and lodgings in Burnley. He had come to make known his suit. The sheer style bowled the household over. Seventy years later my mother retained the most vivid memory of him, a dark, moustached, middle-aged man, as he then seemed to her, of twenty-seven, with polished brown boots and a waistcoat of cushion material and a straw boater which, it was noted, he retained in his lap, eschewing the familiarity of hanging it on one of the ornate knobs of the organ. He was given permission to call again.

About this time my grandfather apparently had a notion to impose his authority on the home. He took on the role of the stern father of Edwardian convention. Watch in hand, he would wait at the door for the breathless arrival of the girls a minute or two after the prescribed time. On Sunday nights he filled the parlour with sanctimonious company from Wesley chapel. There was, however, a countervailing force. Now in his forties, he was beginning to discover in himself a taste and a talent for a wide-ranging social life. His work as an insurance agent was itself a social sort of job and much of it was done in the evening when people came home from the mill, leaving him free to drop into the Liberal club like a man of leisure at odd hours during the day. His skill at billiards reached a new level, his hand at cards sharpened, he was drawn back into politics. My grandmother who had supported his authority in requiring the girls home at nine now waited until midnight for him to arrive covered in blue chalk dust and hot for Irish home rule. On advice she bought him a pipe and some tobacco which was supposed to have the domesticating effect a bone or rug might have for a straying dog. He smoked a few puffs, then rose and repaired to the Liberal club. He had long lived in the country; having hit the bright lights of Bacup, he could not be contained.

Life had changed no less for the girls. Their country upbringing had prepared them for docile domestic service. In Bacup they found themselves among the assertive competent women who were always the greater part of the labour force in cotton and often the backbone of the home. In youth they were brassy girls, later exemplified to the world by Gracie Fields, whose sharp tongues and withering humour drove many a foreman to drink or an early grave. They earned good money. They paid their way. They were not girls to submit to oppression. Abigail began to contend with her father. He retreated. He sacrificed the substance of authority in order to preserve the style. In a town where Christian names were universally used he continued to be referred to with the honorific 'Mister', reverently by his wife, respectfully by the town at large, facetiously by his precocious grandson Stanley Kerry from the age of seven. All that endured of his authoritarian phase was a manner which in time became regal and the Sunday evening gatherings of the righteous in the parlour which continued for some years, partly from habit and partly because on Sunday nights the Liberal club was closed.

The Great War came. Young men went away. Alice, whose education had won her a job on the hoist, went on to become a printer's copy-holder and then an assistant in the firm's stationery shop in place of a man who had gone to the army. She worked an even longer day, twelve hours at least. Closing time varied. Before they locked up she was sent out to be sure the rival stationer's had closed. At weekends the lights of the two shops faced each other out until nearly midnight and Alice on her way home would meet her father who had been turned out of his club, his clothes reeking of cigar smoke and his conversation lively with the contention between Asquith and Lloyd George.

Suddenly the war came close. It had consumed the younger age groups and now the time arrived for Abigail's resplendent fiancé Ben Kerry. The family was appalled that a man of such style might shortly find himself hanging in the barbed wire. The panache of his first appearance had been sustained. He would come swooping over the hill from Burnley on his bicycle at the most unexpected hours. He brought presents. He organised outings. He told stories well and reacted to those of others with a generous tenor chortle. Being beyond his first youth he was able to respond to the parents like a sensible son and to treat the younger sisters with the indulgence of an uncle. Married men of his age were still exempt from military service. It was proposed, I do not know by whom, that he and Abigail should marry forthwith. The Reverend Bert Matthews was got out of bed and the date urgently fixed. Dressmakers were summoned, caterers booked, horses and carriages engaged. Mrs Sephton got a new hat. Mr Sephton presented the happy couple with an insurance policy on Ben's life which their exertions were designed to prolong. Shortly after the wedding the exemption for married men was ended. Mr Sephton was rebuked by his superiors in the Refuge Assurance company, unnecessarily as it turned out. Ben was preserved by his trade. The Royal Flying Corps was looking for his kind of skill to maintain its air frames. It rigged him out with a double-breasted tunic and a field forage cap more suited to his dress sense than army uniform and posted him beyond the sound of guns to Ireland.

He had hardly gone when a greater crisis occurred. My grandfather's concern in the war had so far been confined to consideration of its higher direction and to lending his voice to the community singing in cinemas of war songs suitably bowdlerised for the home front. He was silenced at a stroke. His own calling-up papers dropped through the letter box. It was preposterous. He was too slight to hump a soldier's pack, too short to see over the parapet and he disliked bad language and wet feet. He had not been pampered all his life to drown in a sea of mud. And what to a liberal was even more outrageous, his call-up was not lawful; he was fifty, over the prescribed age. The house was turned upside down in a search for his birth certificate. Prayer was resorted to. The Reverend Bert Matthews was again got out of bed. The doctor was importuned to certify his delicate health and the Refuge Assurance company to testify to his indispensability. A solicitor of libertarian convictions was engaged who alarmingly expressed himself determined to remedy the injustice, however long it might take and if need be posthumously.

In the end the army did not persist, but one Sunday night while the matter still hung in the balance a soldier came to the door whom my grandfather at first took to be an escort sent to arrest him but then recognised as the survivor of five youths from his father's Sunday school class who had joined the East Lancashire regiment together. The soldier asked if he might speak to Alice. He was at twenty a veteran of the Western front, diffident, without opinions, born brave, a son of a different sort of family. Mr Sephton showed him into the parlour where Alice was sitting. Also sitting there were her two sisters and her mother and the Sunday evening gathering from Wesley chapel. Prim faces lit up in query and expectation. The young man blushed to the collar of his tunic and yearned for the sanctuary of the trenches. This was my father Archibald Haworth, a lion thrown to the Christians.

The Forest of Rossendale is an area of high moorland broken by valleys of granite outcrop. It has no history. Nobody ever fought for it and few people lived there. Over the centuries there are records of barely a dozen families. The Haworths were one of them. It must have been a thin living. Moorland grass grows down to the back walls of the houses and there is little bottom land to graze cattle or to grow winter feed for sheep. People survived by digging coal and later by spinning and weaving cotton in the home. These industries, begun for subsistence, became the basis of fortunes. In the late 18th century the desolate valley was

discovered to have everything needed for the factory manufacture of cotton – coal, soft water and a humid climate.
The native families came down from the hills. The names of
some of them rose on mill chimneys. Fortunes ebbed and
flowed. My father was born in 1896 on one of the ebb tides.

His grandfather had been a mechanic of genius who,
banished from the family mills for advocating changed
methods, was heard more sympathetically in the United
States and Germany, and thus embarked on an itinerant and
profligate life supported by his fees and the proceeds of
patents. Whenever he returned to Bacup the town's topers
assembled at the Conservative club and a policeman waited
on the steps to install him in a cab and see him to his
lodging. His son, my grandfather, Frederick Haworth, had
no settled home. He lived for short periods in the grand
houses of relatives, he was boarded out with mill workers,
he slept above the shop of the joiner to whom he was
apprenticed. When he married and moved into the house
that I was to know he might have been expected to cherish
the place. Eventually he did but not until the best years of
life had passed. His behaviour followed the example of the
father he had rarely seen. He was a good workman and
when he was promoted clerk of works at Ross mill, which
was then being built in the middle of Bacup, a genial and
conscientious overseer, absolutely reliable apart from his
drinking sprees. Some Fridays he took his pay and went
neither home nor back to work until he had spent it. He was
not sacked. It was what they expected of any outstanding
tradesman. But at home bills piled up, the furniture was
sold, they sat on orange boxes. Then he would renounce
drink and build a bit more of Ross mill and they would go
round the shops together and refurnish the home. He got
on well with everybody, from his father's old boozing pals
to his wife's friends in the Salvation Army who were
welcomed to the house to practise their choruses and for
their part refrained from attempting to save him. Her picture
of General Booth shared the wall with his of Queen Victoria.
The bailiffs, in propriety, left both portraits whenever they
carted out the rest of the furniture.

Archie was his mother's companion. They shared a love

which neither ever found again. She left for the mill at the end of the street across Burnley road before six in the morning and he as a small child had the kettle on the boil and the table set when she returned with her friends for breakfast at eight. On Monday mornings he rolled up and put away the rag rug. On Fridays before lighting the fire he dug out the week's ashes from the pit below and black-leaded the range. One morning the kettle boiled over into the bucket he had filled with ash, raising a cloud which settled across the room. He was dabbing round with a duster when his mother and her friends arrived. He long remembered her gentle words and sitting through the brief meal with her arm round his shoulder.

They enjoyed social visits to the contrasting homes of the wider family, particularly to those of the many maiden aunts and cousins who lived behind lace curtains on small incomes from the mills. But the backbone of their social life was the Salvation Army. Archie learned the cornet and enjoyed at twelve the delight of playing with the band until the dawn of Christmas Day. On normal Sundays they were out at first light assaulting hangovers with their massed instruments and rollicking choruses.

He went to work as a part-timer at the age of 12, doing half the day in the mill and half at school where the workers were put on the back row and allowed to doze. At the factory they worked barefoot for better balance on floors slippery with oil from the spindles. Archie sorted large bobbins brought by hand truck to the middle of a room and threw them into skips round the walls. He became fast, and proficient enough to hit the skips without looking up. One day he hit the manager who was passing through and laid him out. He left and got a better job at the slipper works as an apprentice in shoemaking. He enrolled for night classes at Waterfoot technical college. He went to a posher Sunday school, leaving the Salvation Army which was opposed to sport, in order to play in the Wesleyans' cricket and football teams. He bought a pink silk tie. He started to make expeditions to Manchester. He went over to Burnley to watch the redoubtable football team that won the F.A. Cup. He remembered walking back over the moors on a spring

evening in a great throng of men, passed occasionally by
cyclists and parties in wagonettes. They strolled in a leisurely
way with the sense that the last match had been played and
summer lay ahead. Many never went again. The season that
had ended was of 1913–14. Their world was about to end.
They walked over the hill and into history.

In my early years everything stopped for two minutes on
Armistice Day, factories, schools, housework, traffic and
people in the street, and the nation stood with heads bowed.
The Great War cast a shadow over the childhood of those
born in its aftermath as though it was the catastrophe we
had actually lived through. Photographs remain in the mind
like memories: the marching columns of glistening capes,
the broken landscape, billets in cellars and half-wrecked
barns, estaminets loud with parley-voo and hoarse with
Woodbines, the line that rose at dawn on the parapet and
diminished and sank in no man's land.

For those who lived through it the dominating memory
was less photogenic: months in which by day nothing on
the battlefield moved and nights spent in digging or in
humping up supplies. My father at seventy could plod away
at a manual task for hours. He handled a spade not as a
gardener might but fluently, with grace, as though it were a
cricket bat or a musical instrument or a weapon. It was once
a weapon, which some men preferred at close quarters to
the bayonet. He seldom spoke about the fighting and never
in detail. He remembered once when they followed in the
barrage and took a section of the enemy line. Australian
cavalry passed through them, bronzed riders on strong
horses, dropping a word as they rode by into the smoke. He
remembered their return, torn men slumped in the saddles,
wounded and riderless horses. It was the way attacks always
ended but memory was deepened by pity and novelty
because of the Australians and the horses.

My father thought that the limitations of the Commander
in Chief, Sir Douglas Haig, sprang from the misfortune of
having passed his formative years in the cavalry. 'He did his
best,' he said. 'After all he was only a horse soldier.' But the
German generals, foot-sloggers and professional to the spike

on their helmets, did no better. Neither side was capable of
a breakthrough. The development of weapons had made
defence impregnable. From October 1914 to March 1918 no
attack or series of attacks moved the front line ten miles in
either direction.

The first volunteers had no idea of what they were letting
themselves in for. Nor had anybody else. The war had
broken out not through intention but through an almost
mechanical escalation of threats; it was an unfortunate confrontation which was expected to be over in a few months
without any noticeable effect on daily life. 'If we are engaged
in war,' the Foreign Secretary Edward Grey said on August
3, 1914, 'we shall suffer but little more than we shall suffer
if we stand aside'. The population had no intention of
standing aside. Lord Kitchener's appeal for volunteers on
August 7 met with a response so vigorous that recruiting
offices were overwhelmed. Football teams, night school
classes, shop floors of workers, office complements of clerks,
villages of farm labourers all went off together and volunteered en masse. Accrington set the pace for East Lancashire;
they raised a battalion in ten days. By the end of 1914 more
than a million men had joined up in Britain.

For my father the war afforded a welcome break from
responsibilities. As seemed usual with the oldest child he
had been treated as a little adult almost from infancy, his
mother's support and comforter. Frank five years younger
remained a child. Then a second brother Walter was born in
1913 and a baby's noise added. The war could not have
come at a better time.

In the group photographs two kinds of faces predominate,
men with sunken eyes and cheeks who look older than
anybody now alive and boys fresh-faced with an innocence
which is also no longer seen. Archie and his pals from the
Sunday school class were of that cherubic appearance and all
of the stocky stature that industry seems to breed. They
were all killed but him. He had no close friends ever again
but in the army he was sustained and kept happy by
comradeship, the impersonal love that nods at every man
and gives him his place, and he enjoyed the quiet popularity
that grows round a reticent and reliable soldier. Whenever

we went to Blackpool on holiday in the 'thirties men with beaming faces would seize him on the promenade and identify themselves with their name and perhaps their unit and often with the name of a place, names on a map that echo in the heart, Ypres, the Menin road, Arras, Bapaume, Passchendaele.

They spoke about it as though it had been a works outing. Daily life in the trenches seems to have held less horror for the rankers than for the educated men who were to write about it ten years later. The troops were of a generation and social class born to rough conditions. A third of the army had lived in slums and most of the rest in their immediate vicinity. Back to back with Archie's home was a tiny house, later converted to a kitchen and a bedroom, in which thirteen people dwelt. The wet and stink of the trenches, the jostle of bodies, the rats in the night were unfamiliar only in degree to most soldiers. The smells which turned delicate stomachs were not much more revolting than those which pervaded whole areas of towns, rising up from industrial processes and effluent, from smouldering coal tips and rivers of deep brown that steamed on winter mornings. Every home had a characteristic smell. Most people smelt of their work.

In 'Death of a Hero' Richard Adlington writes of the torment of the morning wash in water 'cold and utterly filthy'. The troops would not have expected hot water. The only provision for it at home was a tank built into the range and heated by the fire during the hours, few on weekdays, when it was burning. Certainly they were used to clean water but if it came to a choice between cleanness and volume they would choose volume. They had been accustomed to arrive home dirty from industrial processes. A great blowing and splashing wash, stripped to the waist in the scullery, was the ritual end of the working day. The more encrusted workers, coal miners particularly, were scrubbed by their wives, smocked in a clean union shirt and exhibited on the front door step. Men used to such heroic ablutions would have spurned a ration of clean water in a mess tin. My father remembered with disgust a regular soldier who insisted in taking his share in this way and never washed beyond tickling over his features with the brush as the last flourish to his shave. His own habit of vigorous ablution persisted through life. His snorting and blowing roused the household at dawn and left the bathroom walls and window jewelled with droplets as though a large dog had shaken itself.

Even so nobody went to the trenches from choice. Everybody was on the look-out for the chance of being left behind on a cushy number. Archie got one. He was made the company boot repairer on the strength of his uncompleted apprenticeship in shoe-making. He enjoyed three months of clean hot water from the cookhouse in the morning and learned enough about boot repairing to serve as the basis for his future career.

He had several home leaves. At the first his parents were taken aback to see him alive and his brother Frank, a shy youth, deeply embarrassed to be caught wearing Archie's Sunday suit and pink silk tie. It was on his second leave that he paid his formal call on Alice Sephton. He pursued his suit on his return to France by having her photograph printed on a dinner plate surrounded by roses with a background of the town of Ypres. Everybody wanted one. All her friends sent their portraits for transfer to dinner plates, and the traffic only ceased in March 1918 when the German offensive gained momentum and the artist packed his plates and processing and hot-footed it out of town.

The advance was stopped in late summer at the cost to the British of 300,000 casualties. New factors emerged. The mass use of tanks, the first effective weapon of attack, ended the tactical stalemate. The arrival of the Americans, the vanguard of an enormous reserve of manpower, put the ultimate outcome beyond doubt. The German home front collapsed under the privations caused by blockade. British soldiers at the front were only partly aware of these underlying changes. To them the victory they won seemed all of a piece with the war they had fought, the cumulative final reward for the repeated repulse of the enemy and the dogged repetition of their own attacks, costly and useless as they seemed at the time, over four years. The waves no longer shattered on the rocks. The tide rolled in.

More than 700,000 men from the United Kingdom had been killed. One and a half million were badly wounded, of whom many would survive like pale ghosts in the dark streets of the depression. That was not foreseen in the rapturous year of victory parades when the greatest army Britain had ever raised came marching home. Of the armies of the five great European powers that took the field in 1914 it was the only one to endure unbroken in either body or spirit. The Royal Navy was the biggest in the world, the Royal Air Force the most powerful. The empire, its bounds now set wider to embrace a population of 490 million, had become in the words of General Smuts, the Prime Minister of South Africa, 'quite the greatest power in the world'.

Archie Haworth was not by temperament given to public exultation and at 22 he was of the older more staid generation in the army, half of whose soldiers were now under 19. But he returned home at a time of rejoicing when grief was endured secretly and sombre memories pushed out of sight like war medals at the back of a closed drawer. Home was happier. His father had gone off on a trip that finished his appetite for sprees. He had worked in the manufacture of sea-planes on the Isle of Wight and the 60-hour week with a half day off spent in lodgings had nurtured at last a taste for domesticity. He even took an interest in the décor to the extent of fixing an aircraft propellor to the wall opposite the portraits of Queen Victoria and General Booth. He had hoped to add to the exhibition a German helmet Archie brought home but Mr Sephton intercepted it for display in his own parlour. It did not remain there long. The Sunday evening visitors disapproved of what could only be regarded as the booty of war and it was removed to the kitchen where for many years it was utilised inverted as a receptacle for the boot-cleaning tackle.

Alice's career in the stationery shop had blossomed in the war years with the advent of a new proprietor, Mr Robinson, whose deafness proved such a handicap behind the counter that he gave up and made her his manageress and his interpreter. He had never met the previous manager now back from the army and he refused to reinstate him in her place. Nobody felt it was right. Mr Sephton took up the matter. There were earnest consultations. Eventually Mr Robinson agreed to reinstate the manager if Alice would remain until he attuned himself to the new voice. The Reverend Bert Matthews called on the ex-soldier with their findings. The man thanked him, bade him tell Mr Robinson to keep his job, and opened his own newsagent's shop in Burnley road. His manner surprised them.

My father returned in a similar mood. When the manager at the shoe factory demurred at taking him back he abandoned his career in shoe-making. He bought a last and a couple of bends of leather and set himself up as a boot repairer at his parents' home. It went well. He was extremely tidy. He stayed compact in one corner of the room. The cat and kittens occupied the cupboard at the opposite side. Many people called. Reserved by nature and muted at work by the use of his mouth as a nail dispenser, he was an ideal companion for those who wished to talk without the annoyance of being interrupted. He branched out from hob-nailed boots and was soon turning out delicate and shapely repairs of ladies' evening shoes. He moved into the shop I came to know on Burnley road almost opposite the new newsagent's.

It was a good time for business. Cotton boomed. Carts, motor lorries and steam tractors piled high with raw cotton rumbled up in a daily procession from the docks at Liverpool and Salford and returned loaded with bolts of fabric for the markets of the world. Mill owners on the floor of the Manchester cotton exchange found themselves beseiged by customers eager to buy up production for years ahead and ready some of them to buy the mill. Forty per cent of the spinning mills changed hands in 1919. Few doubted that a good time was coming; they could not invest their money fast enough.

Other trades prospered in consequence. Archie's boot repairing business built steadily and the other two suitors of the Sephton girls were re-established in their old jobs. For all of them it was the most affluent time of their life. They bought clothes, they went out in landaus and charabancs, they took railway excursions. Sharing a bed with me in the depression of the 'thirties my uncle Ben remembered those first golden years of peace. 'We were proper high-steppers in those days, Donny.'

Archie's brother Frank stepped out in a way that caused some surprise. He was a morbidly shy youth who would escape from the house whenever visitors arrived, struck speechless no less by Ben Kerry's mature affabilities than by the good cheer of invading Salvationists of his mother's platoon. He was known to be an outstanding student, well thought of by his employers at the shoe factory and his instructors at Waterfoot technical school. He spent his spare time upstairs with his books and seldom went anywhere. It was a surprise when he announced he was going off on holiday – not, it emerged, to Blackpool and not to his mother's relatives in Norfolk. They pressed him no further. He was away a long time. He went to Moscow.

Archie and his friends had taken little cognizance of the revolution. It showed no sign of turning up in booming East Lancashire and they knew nothing of discontents in other parts of the country since tidings of them could only come in newspapers which as old soldiers they mistrusted and seldom read. Frank had better intelligence conveyed through a small committee in a back room in Manchester. They assured him they had a revolution due to start at any time on Clydeside. He was sent back to Bacup to lie low until the ferment should sweep the cotton mills and counselled in the meantime to bone up on theory. This, it turned out, was what he had been doing in his room upstairs when everybody thought he was reading about welts and uppers.

He had in fact finished with his text books on shoe-making and he took them with him to Russia in the hope they might be of service to the people's boot industry. They were received with some surprise but graciously by a minister, one of the pale faces in the group photographs of revolutionaries with beards and concertina trousers who were then enjoying the brief years between a youth of exile in foreign libraries and lodging houses and an eternity in Stalin's limbo. No premonition of this arose to spoil Frank's visit. Ironically it was his own footwear, he later came to think, that disqualified him from continuing a secret role in the Third International. Warned about the winter climate in Moscow, he went in a pair of those hob-nailed boots which it was his brother's speciality to repair. None of the natives was so equipped. They wore galoshes which they discarded at the door and minced round in shoes like dancing slippers. Frank alone could be heard from far off. The two agents of the secret police detailed to see he did not wreck the revolution stayed in the warm and kept him under aural surveillance with the window slightly ajar. Plainly, whatever part he played in the overthrow of capitalism would have to be an open one. A man who would go round in those ringing boots would prosper neither as a mole secretly stirring up the dirt in some factory nor as the quiet sincere citizen doing the donkey work for front organisations devised to ensnare liberals and pacifists. He set himself up openly as a Communist, overcame his shyness through speaking at public meetings, added atheism to his repertoire, and became in time a patient and amiable teacher to any who would hearken, and a ready host to a cosmopolitan stream of party comrades and fellow travellers, odd balls bunkered for a while in Bacup on their unlawful occasions about the world.

Those years of the early 'twenties were still subject to griefs one thinks of as Victorian. A child born to Abbie and Ben died at birth. Evaline, the vivacious middle sister, grew languid, went into a decline and died of tuberculosis. Because of this Archie and Alice postponed their wedding, but it was duly accomplished by the Reverend Bert Matthews in November 1922. I was born in January 1924 and christened by the same divine Donald, after a cricketing parson in the Sunday Companion, as I have already confessed, and Edwin after grandfather Sephton.

6 · MIRACLE AND MIGRATION

In the weeks that we stayed with the grandparents Sephton between giving up the house at Troughgate and moving to Burnley a miracle happened. My grandmother, left alone in the house with my brother Eric during his afternoon sleep, found him on his hands and knees in the cot with his head stuck tight between the bars. She urged him to withdraw. He did not respond. At the age of two he had developed no great grasp of language as a result, it was feared, of the bombardment of his head with wooden building blocks in infancy. What further impairment might be caused by the nutcracker grip of the cot bars did not bear thinking about. She pleaded with him. He grunted. She tried to prise the bars apart, then to twist his neck, then so far as it was possible with one pair of hands to do both together. The bars twanged. The child reverberated but remained stuck. She brought the hacksaw but found it too deep to pass between the bars. She opened the window to call for help but nobody was passing. She sank to her knees and called upon the Lord. The way was made clear: she must arm herself with a tool of greater purpose, the axe. She ran across the side street to the coal place. When she came back into the room Eric rolled his eyes towards her, smiled and withdrew his head.

Faith was fortified and morals drawn. The Lord was indeed a very present help in time of trouble; we should be tested but never beyond our strength; with trust in his guidance we should follow with resolve. It was allowed that there might have been an unexpected access of intelligence in the child. If so, far from invalidating the miracle, it should be seen as an essential element in it, indeed the richest part of its bounty, for he had hitherto seemed quite gormless up to and including the moment when he stuck his head through the bars in the first place. Eric himself in later years had a different explanation. He had been playing up to enjoy the panic. When grandma Sephton returned with the axe he thought she was going to behead him.

It was an exciting place to live, six of us jostling about one small room as though it was Christmas. After tea we sat round the fire waiting for my father to arrive on his motor bike and when he came in glowing from the cold we moved our chairs back so he could join in the conversation as he ate his meal. They were peaceful evenings in the lilt and lull of talk and I tried by concentrating my thought on the beat of the pendulum in the wall clock to hold back the time when the candle would be lighted and I would be led up the winding stone stair to bed. I was not alone in wishing to linger. There was for all in those evenings the sweet sadness of expiring time, for when we went to Burnley we should be distant from my grandparents and, because the Kerrys were also to make the move, they would be left alone. My grandmother put on a show of extra brightness. She was even more shocked and startled at the exaggerated stories my grandfather and I brought back to her. 'That is a caution. Well, I never.' One day on the stairs I heard my grandfather in the room below repeatedly singing a verse of a wistful song:

O, O Antonio, he's gone away
He's left me on my ownio, all on my ownio.

My heart stopped. What was the name? Was it intended to be mine in one of the variations he played upon it? Could real people have their names in songs? Was there a song about our parting? Was he making it up as he sang?

I'd like to meet him with his new sweetheart
Then up would go Antonio and his ice cream cart.

He turned when I reached the foot of the stairs, surprised there was anyone else in the house. For the only time I remember he was unable to find anything to say.

One night I was awakened by the rumble of a conversation which included voices I knew but could not quite place. When I crept down and opened the door of the living room talk ceased. Auntie Abbie and uncle Ben were there in their Sunday clothes. Everybody greeted me with unexpected heartiness and I was ushered off back to bed.

What had happened was that under the pressure of events my grandfather had confessed that his job with the insurance had all but collapsed and that he was badly in debt. It had been a nightmare he had concealed from everybody.

An insurance agent was not exactly an employee of the company. When he took the job he bought a 'book' which was his title to the business of the policies listed therein. On giving up he would sell the book to his successor. Both his commission and the capital he had sunk in the book depended on keeping up the number and value of policies. It was a race to outpace the undertaker, to find new 'lives' to insure as fast as death claimed the old ones. My grandfather was no salesman. Conversation was pleasure; he did not know how to turn it to business advantage. Bad times had him reeling. He treated his family as a strategic reserve, selling a blizzard of policies to them when the influenza epidemics of 1919 and 1925 wiped the names of old customers from his book. All the grandchildren were fixed up with a burial policy at birth. My mother took out an endowment for me which would have been worth four and ten pence at the age of 21. The wider family subscribed. Life policies were taken out by the grandparents Haworth, by uncle Frank and his brood perched at the top of their steep street, and by uncle Ben's maiden sisters who worked at the telephone exchange in St Helens. If we had all gone at one coup, if say the gas had blown up the house with all of us in it on Christmas day, the Refuge would have been ruined. A novel kind of policy was found for grandma Haworth. As a newly apprenticed painter her youngest son Walter was beginning to work up ladders and scaffolds, and the policy would yield a pleasing dividend if he fell off.

The family effort produced harmony at the time and some good bonfires several years later when the policies were burned. The only untoward incident occurred at uncle

Frank's where a comrade, come to run over final details for the overthrow of capitalism, assailed grandfather Sephton. 'Here comes one of their hirelings,' he announced. 'Here comes the bodysnatcher.'

My grandfather let it pass without riposte. It was such a misconception of his role and interests that he could hardly have begun to correct it. The last thing he wished was to see his customers reduced to bodies. 'Lives' they were called in the insurance book and they expired on the page at the very moment they breathed their last. 'Any man's death diminishes me,' the poet proclaimed. My grandfather as his stipend shrank could not have been more aware of shared loss. He could not bear to look at the columns of deaths in the Bacup Times; even to meet someone looking seedy put him off his supper.

Death was one enemy of the book. Poverty was the other. Many people were unable to keep up in the depression of the twenties policies taken out in the post-war boom. At the worst policies could be lapsed and what had been paid in premiums largely or wholly forfeited. But companies were reluctant to apply a sanction which ultimately would have put them out of business. They chivvied the agents to chivvy the 'lives', most of whom were sharp enough to perceive that the agent's interest in keeping the policy going was more desperate than their own and that he would pay the premium out of his own pocket when the threat of lapsing became imminent. Once started on that course there was no going back. In some periods my grandfather paid out nearly as much as he earned in order to sustain his book and keep his job.

He did not speak of his deepening anxiety. He borrowed from a moneylender who came to the door when he was out and demanded repayment from my grandmother. My grandfather denied to her that he had borrowed the money and went and borrowed some more in order to repay it secretly. He was accelerating down a steepening slope when they learned that the two branches of their family were leaving Bacup. It was one of those coincidences which are the signposts of destiny. Lies become pointless, events out of control resolve themselves in an unforeseen way. My grandfather's job in insurance was finished. They would have to sell up their home to pay his debts. They had nobody to go to except family. When we moved, they moved. For the next ten years they had no home of their own but lived alternately with the Kerrys and with us. There were no jobs for a man over sixty. My grandfather made no attempt to find one. He was not dispirited by defeat. He had enjoyed the sociability of the job. The only aspect he disliked was the work. Freed of that, he embarked on a career of leisure which he pursued with talent and success until his death at the age of 79.

7 · THE PROMISED LAND

Burnley is the largest of five stone-built towns narrowly strung along the valley of the river Calder. To the south its streets rise to high moorland, to the north green fields undulate past woods and villages to the foot of Pendle hill. Beyond lies Ingleborough and Penyghent in the limestone country of the Yorkshire dales. There are few streets in Burnley from which the hills can not be seen or reached on foot. People can breathe. In 1929 it was still the biggest cotton weaving town in the world. A hundred mill chimneys churned out a cumulus of smoke which permanently overhung the valley. The Leeds and Liverpool canal wound through. A huge gasometer stood where the houses ended and the fields began, like a squat and patient giant set to keep the place under scrutiny. This was to be the promised land, and so it was for me. I cannot imagine a better place to grow up.

The weeks before we moved were full of excitements. We packed the crockery in tea chests. The clock was carefully taken down, leaving a pattern of its shape on the wallpaper. The hanging plant behind the front door we left for the next people. No mention was made of all the things that would be taken to the saleroom to pay my grandfather's debts, but they reckoned up many times with their shaky arithmetic and rejoiced that they would be able to keep the secretaire and the mahogany table which had been wedding presents to both of them and a chest of drawers which her employers had given my grandmother at marriage and which eventually she was to leave to me. My grandfather sang, freed from

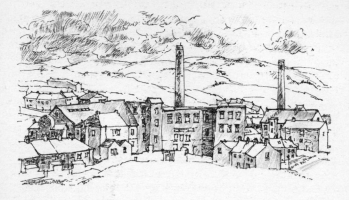

the weight of failure and deceit and from paid employment which in its different forms had been burdensome to him from the time his own trade as a watchmaker collapsed twenty years previously. Their children would provide subsistence. The only money they would have until he was sixty-five would be the ten shillings a week of my grandmother's pension. It proved to be more than adequate to sustain an eventful life.

The prospect of migration cheered uncle Ben. Auntie Abbie would give up work. He would save his daily bus fare to Burnley and be able to go home to his dinner. He announced that it would be a hundred per cent better in every conceivable way. They found a house to rent in Irene street. It had an unpaved carriageway where tradesmen's carts rocked through puddles but it housed distinguished citizens, including Jack Yates, retired comedian, churchwarden and leading light in the Labour party, and it commanded at one end a prospect of the parkland of Towneley hall and beyond of the cliffs of the glacial valley that runs to Todmorden. Uncle Ben said it was where the aristocrats used to live, an unsurpassable abode ideally situated.

For my parents also the promise was bright. They had intended to make the move since my father had sold his business and gone to work at Burnley Co-op eighteen months earlier. Now they had no doubt that he had done the right thing. His management of the branch shoe shop at Harle Syke had been successful and he had been promoted to a bigger branch in Accrington road. He had two bench men and a clogger under him and this, he was assured, was only a first step in the progress the management expected him to make.

It was a high point. My parents bought a square of carpet pungent with newness and we crawled across it in line abreast, palms down to smooth out the wrinkles. I believe I remember them standing back to admire it, and the echo of their pleasure in the room still empty of furniture sounds in my memory now like a reverberation from a different dimension of time. Twice their age, I look back at these young people, as such never known to me, looking forward to a future in time now long expired. In the confused moment between sleep and waking I am alarmed that I might have failed to recognise them, contrite at my superior knowing, and regretful that I cannot warn them to temper their hope.

The stone house we rented was at the end of a row with hen pens opposite the front door and Lionel street school opposite the windows of the gable. The big bedroom was never furnished but used as a playroom. The room beyond it contained a bath which was made up as a bed for me during the visits my grandparents paid us from their more usual abode with the Kerrys at the other end of town. Living in Burnley yielded my grandfather the boon of being within reach of a first eleven Lancashire League cricket match every Saturday of the summer, alternately at Turf Moor and Lowerhouse. A narrow path ran for a mile through the hen pens and fields from our front door to Lowerhouse cricket ground. There were hundreds of pens, divided by wilting wire-netting and containing ramshackle tarred huts patched up with pieces of oilcloth and rusted tin sheets bearing the remains of advertisements for Oxo, Frys' Five Boys' chocolate, Colman's mustard and Reckitts' blue. The hens scratched outside. The huts were inhabited by old men who on days of extreme heat slightly opened the door permitting an exhaust of tobacco smoke to roll out under the lintel. They were there every day, turned out as soon as they finished breakfast so wives or daughters could get on with the housework. The owners of the pens seem to have accepted the use of their huts as asylums as an obligation inherent in poultry keeping. They were mainly younger men and you would see them plodding to the pen at morning and evening clasping their lapels, with the handles of buckets, one containing water and one containing slops, over the crook of their arms. The old men arrived after the morning visit and had gone by the time the pen keeper came again in the evening, apart from those who delayed as long as possible a return to an embattled hearth and some of the older ones who forgot where they lived. They helped to lock up the hens for the night.

During the day the old men were under obligation to see that the pen gate was kept closed. You would not know they were there. They lay low, holed up in different hen cotes on different days, in case the women who banished them came to retrieve them for some unforeseen job. They kept their heads down. The pens were as devoid of human movement as a Great War battlefield in a lull. You heard only the cluck of the hens and the distant hum of the mills and clank of railway waggons. But the moment you went in, say to retrieve a ball, doors flew open and voices erupted, croaking, protesting, ordering, rebuking, threatening, the whole Thesaurus of abuse and admonition, from which you would devine their wish that the gate should be closed on departure and never reopened.

They also had an obligation not to set the place on fire but this they kept less well. In the hot days of summer one in the maze of pens would go up as though an incendiary bomb had landed. Old men and hens came fluttering and squawking out of the flame and smoke. The fire was assaulted with oaths and coats and sacks. They formed human chains with buckets and drenched each other. Firemen in rubber boots stumbled among the loose stones of the paths shaking the kinks out of their hose, then on came their powerful jet. It wrecked the hen cote and left its fowl

bedraggled and its old men sodden and dripping at the edge
of a shallow lake.

Knowing of the scorn felt for foreigners, I allowed it to be
understood at my new school that we had been resident
hitherto not in some alien place but in a different district of
Burnley. This was not difficult to put across. Nine houses
out of ten were let on a weekly rent and everybody was
constantly on the move. It was a universal hobby. The
present-day upwardly mobile are stagnant by comparison.
Some gypsies stayed longer. It made more sense in buying
furniture to consider how it might look on the back of a
coal cart rather than how well it might go with a room. The
population did not so much reside in the town as swirl
around it, fish in a pool rather than vegetables in a garden.
Children were constantly changing school so it was easily
possible to disguise from my new school mates that I was
an immigrant.

Then one morning, called up for some reason to the
platform during prayers, I became aware of the Achilles'
heel of my deception. All the boys in the singing rows wore
striped elastic belts fastened by a metal buckle S-shaped in
the form of a snake. Behind each snake was a flap of belt
material so the stripes ran uninterrupted behind the buckle. I

had no such flap. My buckle fastened across a gap in which the grey of my trousers showed. Theirs were Burnley belts and mine, now exposed to the gaze of the whole school, was a Bacup belt. I turned sideways looking down on the hymn singers over my shoulder like a figure on an Egyptian tomb. For the prayer I contrived a ferocious scowl to direct at any boy who might commit the blasphemy of raising his eyes. The headmistress's short address I heard with my hands resting over my paunch like a comfortable alderman. Longer-term measures would have to be thought of. I never considered asking for a new belt. Everything was worn until it fell to pieces. The Bacup belt would be worn by me until it could be adjusted no further then with diminishing elasticity by my brother until his trousers fell. In the middle of the night I thought of wearing it back to front or of crayoning a piece of paper to place behind the buckle but in the light of morning neither of these measures seemed practical. Then in a moment of inspiration I hit on the explanation that I had accidentally snipped off the flap in the normal course of making passes with the scissors. In the end I was disappointed that the days went by unchallenged and that this compelling explanation never reached the public it deserved.

My trouble with clothes was not ended. I had accepted out of loyalty to my father's trade the long disappointment and the disadvantage at football of wearing boots when everybody else wore clogs but now I was threatened with an outfit which promised to be a repeat of the velvet suit and straw hat which had exposed me to hatred, ridicule and contempt at Troughgate. A professionally taken photograph arrived in the post of cousin Stanley, wearing a double-breasted tweed coat with a velvet collar and a cap to match watched from a backdrop of misty Scotland by understandably shocked Highland cattle. With the photo-graph came lengths of cloth, out of which similar ensembles might be fashioned for Eric and me. The cloth was spoken of as bolts which I thought had something to do with bolts from the blue or with thunderbolts, meaning an alarming blow of fate. I was required to write two letters of thanks to auntie Abbie, one to be signed by myself, the other to bear my brother's mark.

A lady dressmaker in a house up Alder street brought out a pattern book containing photographs of youthful prigs. She tried to coax us to choose between different types of buttons and half belts and gave us many fittings. She worked round us on her knees keeping up a mocking patter, 'My word, you will be a big boy,' thrusting pins into us the while. The matching caps were too small on delivery and shrank when rain seeped through to their cardboard peak. They permitted us only two expressions, the constant amazement of raised eyebrows or a permanent scowl. We could perform variations on a theme, both of us in wonderment together, both of us glowering, the one amazed and the other frowning. These were private performances done in the sanctuary of the home. Outside, we stole furtively about the streets keeping to the shadows.

My ensemble in fawn was completed in time for my sixth birthday. At Claremont Sunday school I sneaked into the cloakroom fast and discarded it. The cap peak left a weal across my forehead but nobody seemed to notice it and in honour of my birthday I was bidden to stand facing the class to benefit from a custom which was new to me. At a note from the piano the children sang:

A birthday greeting to you, dear.
May you be happy all the year.

Dear? It was not a word we used. But I had come across it in books which carried illustrations of children indistinguishable from those in the dressmaker's pattern book. The allusion was unmistakeable. They knew. If God could see you under the table, his servants would be sharp enough to spot you between the gate and the cloakroom and, following his known malevolence, would not think twice about incorporating a humiliating reference into the birthday serenade.

If you are sweet and kind and true
Our Father's smile will rest upon you.

Nothing offensive there. Perhaps dear was just one of those words like 'ere and joyous and eventide which were used in hymns and books but not in speech. A little girl smiled at me. She wore a white dress with blue polka dots and matching knickers and sang with her head a little on one side, articulating the words like women who used lip speech in the mills.

> And He will be so glad to see you
> Growing up His child to be.

I smiled back at her. She made a pleased little movement of her shoulders, and came to the refrain:

> A birthday greeting to you, dear,
> May you be happy all the year.

I froze. 'Dear' I had come to terms with, but there was a horrifying embellishment, a prefix she sang with an intake of breath, 'a-dear.' Mockery. I was too rattled to see who else might be taking part in the outrage, but the little girl in the spotted dress was clearly the ringleader. Her articulation, overemphasized through the verses, was grossly exaggerated to drive home the insulting prefix with each refrain.

It taught me lasting lessons about the nature of women and the folly of amiability. I suppose a glowering manner would have developed even without the cap. My brother similarly accoutred grew up without a frown. He took to putting on his cap front first, raising his eyebrows in a look of blank surprise. He won early popularity for his likeness to Stan Laurel and as the years passed he learned to temper his expression to one of receptive pleasure which served him well in his career as a salesman. As for me, in those simple days when Dr Freud could not have kept body and psyche together from his British earnings, incipient paranoia remained unrecognised, unnamed and unchecked, an omission which enabled me to sail through life without experiencing any failure that was not clearly caused by a conspiracy of other people.

I began to be taken to Sunday school on Wednesday evenings, which struck me as anachronistic. It was not for religious instruction but to participate in 'practice'. We sang hymns or songs and pranced round, and selected individuals recited doggerel. Prompted by my mother, I learned the choruses in the script which had been stickily printed in purple ink by transfer from a jelly. I began to enjoy practice and to think of myself as a reasonable practitioner. Nothing of the sort. The teacher summoned my mother and explained that the time was now getting near (for what?) and I still could not skip. Girls hovered and listened. The other scholars, she went on, learned to skip as soon as they came to Sunday school. Perhaps that was not done in Bacup?

A couple of months previously I would have been paralysed. But experience had hardened me; exposure and insult could happen at any time without provocation or warning. My mother said I had worked hard at learning the words. The teacher said she couldn't give me an individual speaking part. My mother said she didn't mean that. Because, the teacher said, the speaking parts had already been allocated to little girls and boys who skipped well last year. They had learned their lines, page boy suits in green had been made for the boys and their parents were very much looking forward to 'the day'.

On the way home, holding on to the handle of Eric's push chair, I began at last to get an inkling of what was afoot. 'Practice' was not an end in itself. It was directed towards 'the day'. Nobody had explained that to me. No doubt it was an accidental omission, but there had been deliberate concealment of detail in which my mother had colluded by evading questions about the cream coloured linen she had been stitching on a borrowed Singer sewing machine. The green page boy suits the teacher had mentioned would be worn by the boys with speaking parts. The rest, prancers of the chorus, would be dolled up in similar outfits but of the cream material whose fashioning I could hear as I lay abed of nights. On 'the day' an audience of parents, aunts and grandparents would assemble in the hall and we up on the stage would perform the assinities of the purple script. The legs of my combinations would show beneath my page boy trousers. The teacher would announce that I could not skip because I came from Bacup. I expressed a wish to resign.

My mother thought it better to accept the challenge and surprise everybody by learning to skip before the next practice. She would coach me though not herself an accomplished skipper. Evidently skipping was not a part of Christian instruction in Whiston either; it must be peculiar to the Burnley faithful. We hoofed round the echoing spare room together. Eric chained up in the corner roared with laughter and reduced us both to tears. My father when he came home restored our smiles by demonstrating different kinds of skipping and for my encouragement spoke of such manly troupes of skippers as Cossacks and footballers in training. The next day he brought home for me a marble the size of a billiard ball and for my mother an unbreakable tea pot. He sauntered into a game of football I was playing with boys on the cinders between the houses and the hen pens and ran round us once or twice on twinkling feet. He then conducted a training session with and without the ball, leading to the kind of skipping required for 'the day'. He said the teacher would be very surprised how quickly I had learned. She was not. She did not turn a hair. I marvelled at the composure with which she accepted the frustration of her plot to bring about my public humiliation.

My father in those days, 1930, was a smiling young man, dark, of short athletic build and with a manner that was direct and slightly diffident. I saw little of him. He worked till eight on most evenings and was free on Tuesday after-noons when I was at school but not on Saturdays. I never went anywhere with him alone. On Sundays after Sunday school the family of us went down through the fields to the river Calder. The whole town turned out wearing best clothes. My father had a bowler hat and the gold watch and chain his father had sent him for his twenty-first birthday in France. My mother held his arm. We were not allowed to kick stones, climb gates or cross streams by stepping stones. The concern was for Sunday clothes, social propriety and Sabbath keeping in that order. But the Sabbatarian principle was strong. We spent no money on Sundays. What went into the box for Jesus was not regarded as expenditure. We

observed the wicked coming out of shops breaking chocolate
wrappers or licking ice cream. Some people who smoked
Woodbines all week bought Players or Capstan on Sunday,
the kind of ostentatious defiance that brought desolation to
the tribes of Israel. But we could have done with a bottle of
pop. One forgets the acuity with which thirst and hunger
are felt in childhood. Suffering, Oscar Wilde said, is one
long moment. In childhood indeed it is. Attention concen-
trates itself wholly on the pain and the measurement minute
by minute of the period through which it will have to be
endured. My mother spoke of a Sunday when as a child in
Knowsley park her thirst had driven her to pick up an
orange rotting on the ground. In memory it seems that Eric
and I were permanently close to that extreme although our
expeditions seldom lasted two hours.

Back home we drank cold water until our heads ached
and my parents bustled round like professional waiters to
get the tea for which we were desperately hungry. There
were things we never had on other days, tinned salmon and
salad, pineapple chunks or jelly and custard, home-baked
sandwich cake, and in winter celery that arrived with slivers
of ice on an oblong plate. We would ask a blessing. Eric at
the beginner's stage would recite:

> Bless this food which now we take
> And keep us good for Jesus' sake.

I had advanced to a proclamation which included the vocabulary and invertions of a proper prayer:

> Sanctify, O Lord, we beseech Thee,
> These Thy productions to our use
> And us to Thy service
> For Christ's sake, Amen.

We all said 'Amen' together and smiled at each other, then
my mother filled and passed out the teacups and the tea
began. We concentrated our best eating into Sunday with
bacon and egg for breakfast and a roast at dinner, and in
those prosperous days there were grown-up sweets, sugared
almonds or wrapped caramels, in the wooden bonbon dish.

Weekdays were thinner. Perhaps bacon or an egg for

breakfast but not both. The Monday dinner, prepared quickly in the clutter and steam of washday, was a stew called lobby or scouse. Part of the remains of the Sunday joint went into it. The rest went into a deep potato pie which on Tuesdays was brought to the table puffing like a locomotive through a pot funnel in its crust. It was the finest repast to be encountered this side of paradise, preferable even to the Sunday roast, partly because of the merits of the dish and partly because it recurred on a day unblighted by piety. Moreover, being half-day closing, it was the one weekday my father had dinner with us. Food always tasted better in his company. He ate with zest, tackling the meal in his workmanlike way, graceful with knife and fork, wiping up every last drop of gravy with bread and leaving the plate as spotless as though a dog had been at it. We imitated him. We held our plates upside down to show how clean they were. It was a welcome development. It weaned Eric from the habit of indicating he had had enough by flinging about the room what remained in his dish. There had been no anticipating him. Without warning he would whoop like a Red Indian and the sideboard mirror would be splattered as though somebody had opened up with a machine gun. Lumps of bread sodden in milk hit the window and, slowly sliding, blanked out half the light of day. Books were consulted, the case was mentioned to the doctor, crones came and prescribed cruel remedies suitable for cats and ravens. The race to show a clean plate eventually cured him. He had a yellow enamel dish with a picture of a black boy and a black sheep on the bottom. The boy and the sheep disappeared, scoured up with bread and eaten. It seemed the lesser evil.

We had fruit pies after the potato pie on Tuesday and again at tea. It was the pastry-baking day and most of the pies were eaten within hours of coming hot from the oven. Only one pie usually survived to Wednesday along with the little pastry men with currant eyes and buttons we were allowed to make ourselves. There was a strong tradition among industrial workers to concentrate the good things into a couple of blow-outs and let the rest of the week take care of itself. When times got bad they devoured two enormous meals within six hours on Christmas Day and half-starved for the next twelve months. It was quite at odds with my mother's country-bred frugality and she was alert for any opportunity to make her pies last. She could not have baked on an extra day because that would have meant heating the oven for a less than full load and in any case the baking days were fixed in a pattern of housework which was nowhere prescribed but universally followed and which she would not have felt free to vary. Why not? Well, in a society informed by Nonconformity and disciplined by industry there were no actions free from moral imperatives and no persons free from scrutiny. By whom? Each other. I have been told that as late as 1900, though admittedly in Padiham, people who went out courting on Friday nights were pursued by spontaneous demonstrators banging buckets and shovels to bring them back to their duty of cleaning the house. No doubt there were elements of sport and malice in this, but the instruction my grandparents gave my mother about her conduct as a housewife was entirely solemn. Grandfather Sephton warned her never to fail, as grandma Sephton had never failed, to change out of her working clothes before her husband came home, and I remember my mother, when she had been delayed by a job going wrong or one of us being ill, rushing from bathroom to bedroom like a late actress desperate to be ready for the rise of the curtain.

In the mills workers were taught as soldiers are taught to do jobs reliably by following the same unvarying pattern. In the home women who did not stick to a fixed routine of domestic work would be suspected of skimping it. Moreover diligence had to be apparent and persistent. For a woman to sit down and read the newspaper during the morning would have been as outrageous as for a minister to knock off for a smoke in the middle of his sermon. Nothing more hurtful could be said about a woman than that she was 'not too particular'. The duty of keeping the home spotless and having meals ready on the dot was, as far as I can judge, wholly and unresentfully accepted by women. It was they who exerted on each other and on their daughters a pressure to comply as gentle, pervasive and invisible as the pressure of the atmosphere on the surface of the earth. Women who went out to work had a different pattern of housework to follow and their children were brought into the routine at an early age. Menfolk usually did nothing even if they were on the dole and at home all day.

Keeping a house clean was an endless battle against the soot in the atmosphere and the cinders we trod in from the many unpaved streets. Children's hands and knees were always black and their blouses clean only for the first half hour of the day. Washing was laborious. Successive loads of heavy clothes were grappled with in the tiny kitchen. They were sloshed and soaked and possered in the tub, scrubbed on the washboard, simmered in the little gas-fired boiler, rinsed, then purged of grey cascading water between the wooden rollers of the mangle. The yard was too small to dry sheets. After the tradesmen's carts had gone, lines were strung across the back street and fastened round the drain pipe of the house opposite. They were vulnerable. A prop might be dislodged by a child or the wind, causing the washing to sag against walls or trail in the cinders; footballs could leave the imprint of their segments; squalls of soot struck like grapeshot. In winter the house was steamy half the week from drying the washing round the fire.

My grandmother had scattered wet tea leaves to lay the dust and swept the carpet with a stiff brush. My mother got a Ewbank when they went to Manchester for a shoe and leather exhibition. She said, rather defensively, that it was a boon but admitted it did not clean the carpet nearly so well, so sometimes on Tuesday afternoons when my father was at home we had a ceremony of setting the furniture back on the surrounding oilcloth, lugging the carpet out and beating it on the sagging clothes line. Clouds of dust rolled over the walls to refute and choke anybody who might have thought that people with Ewbanks were not too particular. On the bedroom day, Thursday, my mother took the rugs out and banged them against the outhouse walls.

It was not enough to keep dirt at bay. Furniture, wood-work and oilcloth had to be polished. Every home had its individual smell, acutely noticeable to a child, but the basis of them all was Mansion Polish. On Wednesdays my mother cleaned the strip of stairs carpet with tea leaves and hand brush, and we polished the sides of the treads, taking care not to smear the carpet and to leave no trace of polish in the ornamental pattern of the metal stair clips. Who, it might be asked, would notice them in the dark? There was a short answer to that. God.

Shopping took ages. Nobody had a refrigerator to keep things and in any case few had the money to buy except in the smallest quantities for immediate need. Grocers spent hours weighing out half-pennyworth's of ingredients that would now come already mixed in big packages. Every day something had to be bought that the tradesmen with carts either did not bring or charged too much for. Women would go to several shops of the same sort chasing the lowest price for each item, wait while the weighing was done, then rush to the next shop, conscious of time passing and the obligation to have the dinner on the table at twelve. It was not done to stop and talk in the street. Accosted by old people who had lost sense of time, women would say they were 'pushing'. Of any housewife who did stop it was said that she 'would talk all day'. It was nearly as bad as being 'not too particular' and indeed possibly evidence of it.

One effect of the weight of housework in those days before detergents and electrical gadgets was that nobody who went out to work chose to live alone. Young people stayed with their parents until marriage. Bachelors and widowers unless they were very poor engaged housekeepers. Widows depended pro tem on neighbours and sisters, and kept a sharp eye out for an uncaptured male. Women with invalid husbands, of whom there were many in the wake of the Great War, worked themselves to death.

After the glory of the potato pie and the fruit pies on Tuesday, Wednesday was a wretched come-down – neck of mutton in which scraps of meat had to be patiently separated on the plate from splintered bone. On Thursday we had tripe and onions, on Friday liver and bacon, and on Saturday sausage and mash, a meal which for the third time in seven days was invested with the aura of a feast, though more in celebration of the free day than of the food itself. Saturday was the second baking morning of the week, of cakes for

Sunday. We greased the tins and were allowed to eat the remains of the cake mixture which we scraped from the bowl with a wooden spoon.

The bulk of all the dinners, even Sunday's, was potato, the bulk of all the other meals was bread. Meat and vegetables at dinner, jam and butter at tea were for flavouring not substance. My mother believed that my father took the precept that man does not live by bread alone far too literally. Nurtured in the more prodigal habits of his childhood home and the army, he dived into the jam as though the ration for a whole regiment had just been brought up the line. My mother forbade us to comment but she herself sometimes gasped audibly when he slapped it on like mortar on a brick.

We usually had jam or syrup for tea. Sometimes we had a boiled onion, which was very good, brought to the table in a bowl and well peppered; and sometimes toast. It was permissible to finish off with jam and buttered bread after an onion but not to have both jam and butter on toast. Sometimes my mother made chips and sometimes as a special treat we would buy a load of proper chips from the shop on Padiham road where women from the mills conducted mimed conversations through the sizzle and steam. For supper we had pobbies, bread in warm milk, and thus ended days which extended into years of living largely on carbohydrates. We grew up strong and fit and survived years in which the potato and the loaf were held in low esteem to see nutritional theory catch up with common habit and the rich, coked up with fats and proteins, take expensive cures in which they are restricted to the fodder of our frugal childhood.

8 · ON TWO WHEELS

In truth we felt to be very well off. One day we all got dressed up and took the tram to the studio in Yorkshire street where Stanley had been photographed in front of the Highland cattle. Eric and I were seated in tandem on a short upholstered bench so that we had to turn our heads to face the lens, which the photographer said would make us look alert and intelligent. He wore pince-nez glasses and a check waistcoat and his hair stood in wisps from diving in and out of the black cloth tent that hung over his camera. His art was the antithesis of passport photography which exposes the inherent criminality of its clients. He made angels who yet bore some ressemblance to his subjects. The proofs so moved my mother that she offered a prayer of gratitude for us.

On summer evenings we went to meet our father who came from work smiling through the flecks the machines threw on his face. One evening he appeared wheeling a child's bicycle. My tricycle was formally handed on to Eric who as the younger child seldom got anything new. My father taught me to ride, striding along with his hand gripping the back of the saddle, and he demonstrated to a circle of children the use of the two spanners from the saddle pouch. He tightened the brake rod couplings, re-set the tension of the chain and adjusted the height of the handlebars and saddle. The children asked him what age each saddle height was intended to suit and one boy asked him how high the saddle would have to go for somebody of seventy.

My father raised the stem to its full height, making the
machine look like a giraffe. Everybody went off laughing.

The bicycle was more than a toy. It conferred on me an
identity, the possessor of a bicycle, a cyclist. The wheel
spokes sang to me in school and the freewheel ratchet ticked
in the drowsy minutes before sleep. I showed off my speed
and control to anybody who might spare a glance. Falls I
passed off as a normal hazard of the cyclist, trivial and
painless. I cultivated an insouciance which held back tears
and disguised limps. Then one day I came a real cropper.
My mother sometimes took us on a shopping trip in the late
afternoon, Eric in his push chair with the purchases wedged
in round him, I on my bike. I turned slightly ahead of her
from Padiham road on to the steep descent of Alder street
and gathered speed. I saw the dressmaker at her window.
Other faces appeared at doors and windows. Pedestrians
turned. The wheels bumped rapidly over the joins in the
pavement. I could hear a motor lorry hidden by the school
building but approaching the corner below. My mother
shouted. Old men gaped. Old ladies spoke rebukes. I
squeezed the brake and shot over the handlebars.

People picked me up. Others consoled my mother. Some
followed us into the house. The bicycle, handlebars and
front wheel askew, was dumped in the yard. Auntie Nellie
Battersby who had come to live in Padiham road heard I
had been killed and arrived wearing her black bonnet. I
brooded. An old lady said it was nervous reaction. It wasn't.
It was the sober knowledge that this fall could not be
dismissed with bravado; it was a floundering cropper caused
by incompetence and panic, and it so jolted the smooth
working of my paranoia that I was unable to think of
anybody else to blame. Moreover there were deadly witnesses. Two girls in my class at school were watching when
I was prised out of the wall.

When my father arrived home he came up to my bedroom.
'I hear you had a spill,' he said. That put it into some sort of
perspective. Perhaps the little girls, though staring, had not
actually noticed. Perhaps they had noticed but would forget
as you might a poem or the multiplication tables. They
did not. They came towards me across the school yard,

accumulating followers. 'People shouldn't ride bikes down steep hills,' one of the girls said. I made a gesture intended to mean that I was the kind of cyclist who rode bikes anywhere.

'You fell off coming down Alder street last night.

'No,' I said, 'I didn't.'

'Oo, you big liar. He did, didn't he?' she asked the other girl.

'It weren't me,' I said.

'It were,' she shouted, 'you was coming down Alder street and you tumbled off your bike.'

Tumbled. An infant word, deadly. 'It weren't me,' I said in desperation. 'I weren't coming down Alder street and I didn't fall off my bike.'

The onlookers, bored, began to drift away. The girls put on a look of wounded reproof which mothers assumed when they were 'vexed', but there was no more to be said. It was all over. I had got away scot free, my sporting reputation barely blemished. I saw that the most ingenious excuse would not have served nearly so well. I had discovered the principle of the big lie, two or three years I like to think before Dr Goebbels.

I went down with measles. When I ran out of reading my mother dug out some old books which were kept in a tea chest. They included her Sunday school prizes, slim volumes from which sombre and oppressive clouds arose. Their picture of life as suffering redeemed in passing by small joys and ultimately by salvation was startlingly new to me. Bible stories, as told in Sunday school, were safe and happy. Nursery rhymes and fairy stories could be alarming but usually ended well. The Victorian past, as recounted by grandfather Sephton, was a time of teeming incident, patriotic and temperance songs in the streets, election campaigning, close encounters of many kinds. Here was a different account. The poor, as Oscar Wilde said, were always burying their relations. The authors of Sunday school prize books emphasized the point for the instruction of little children and hammered home the morals to be drawn.

The books were by no means lacking in incident. 'Dust,

Ho! or Rescued from a Rubbish Heap', which I have kept
and treasure, encompasses in sixty-four small pages a plot
sufficient for a novel. We first meet the father, Benjamin, a
scavenger, 'ragged, gray and shrunken, bent with hunting
among rubbish', who likes a drop. Paid for his pickings by
'the old Jew Solomon', he proceeds to the pub and arrives
home in a bad temper. His wife and two daughters huddle
together in the bare room and his wailing son Davy lies in a
wooden box. There is nowhere for Benjamin to sit. 'With a
muttered oath he seized the wooden box and turning it
savagely on one side shook out the contents, then slamming
it down bottom upwards he seated himself upon it. "Now
then I've stopped your noise," he said with a jeer.'

Davy was a 'lovely child with brown hair clustered in
soft silky curls on his forehead,' but at the age of four unable
to walk. 'He had just lain and suffered.' But things take an
upward turn. Davy's older sister Carrie, out gathering rags,
is given three pence by a housemaid. Fuel is bought, a fire
lit and Davy, restored to his box, is placed to enjoy its
warmth. Now the first of the good tidings arrive. His other
sister Janet, turning over the contents of Carrie's sack, spots
a printed picture 'the like of which she had never seen . . .
A group of women with babies in their arms stood round a
man who, seated on a stone in their midst, appeared to have
just drawn a little boy towards him. Underneath was written
"Suffer little children to come unto me" and underneath
that the hymn:

> Here's a message of love
> Come down from above
> To invite little children to Heaven:
> In God's blessed Book
> Poor sinners may look
> And see how all sin is forgiven.

Janet awards the piece of paper to little Davy who,
although suitably grateful, is in the dark about its meaning.
Elucidation is at hand. Miss Ellen, the employer of the
housemaid who gave Carrie three pence, arrives with the
mission of uplifting the family. With little Davy in her arms
and the sisters and their mother gathered round, Miss Ellen

'told the old, old story taking for her text the words under the picture', reducing the girls to tears of gratitude at the revelation and their mother to tears of repentance at having neglected the faith. But Miss Ellen brought a more tangible bounty. 'It was no less than to take Carrie home with her to train as a servant'.

But little Davy is more groggy than the reader had been informed. In the excitement he is dispatched in a subordinate clause. 'So one morning, when Davy's life was ebbing away, Carrie made her preparations for leaving home.' Davy passes. His mother, 'bending her steps towards the public house her husband frequented', is run over and killed by a fire engine.

Carrie moves to work at a house in the country, 'where the roses and honeysuckle peeped in at the window', and Miss Ellen arrives to offer Janet a similar situation. 'At first Janet's eyes glistened with delight but presently they filled with tears and she shook her head, "I cannot leave father" is all that she answered. "I want you above all to do God's will, whatever that is," Miss Ellen replied. "If you ask Him to show what His will is, He will make your path plain."'

Janet stays. Miss Ellen comes up trumps for a final time with a down payment on a business for her. 'So as the spring advanced Janet was supplied with neat clothing and capital to start as a flower girl, and day after day found her sitting or standing patiently at a corner with a basket of sweet-smelling flowers; and it was wonderful how many people looked out for and bought of the girl who was always so gentle and pleasant . . . One thing filled her with joy – her father entirely gave up the drink.'

The book, I saw from the label stuck inside the cover, was presented to my mother by the Lord Mayor of Liverpool for regular attendance at Whiston Wesleyan Sunday school during 1904. She was then six. I was bothered to know what she knew of this downtrodden life I had not hitherto heard about. It was long ago, she said, and in cities. The books had been written by people in their old age and distributed as Sunday school prizes by old habit. My grandfather who forbade his daughters to curtsy when the squire's daughters passed on horseback apparently took issue with the social implications of the works but not, it seems, with other aspects. Thinking about it, my mother said it was a general practice in religious families in those days to frighten children in order to make them more grateful for their blessings. Even her own gentle mother had played an ambiguous game in which she pretended not to recognize her. My mother thought it significant that the chapel had been the scene of her recurrent dream in which she glided down the steps into the darkness where the devil waited.

It was a relief to turn to the breezy and extrovert books awarded to my father by the Salvation Army which were inspired by a quite different concept of spreading the good tidings. 'Brave Sons of the Empire' had on its front cover an illustration of a soldier with a walrus moustache and a scarlet tunic advancing through palm fronds with bayonet fixed. The chapters were divided between accounts of those brave sons who brought salvation to the heathen with the Good Book and those who brought it with a taste of the Gatling gun, a twin-track approach which in the gentle days of 1930 was no more to be contemplated than keeping infants in orange boxes.

I made these excursions into imperial and social history while enjoying the luxury of illness. As I lay warm in bed I would hear the other children going to school in the morning and the familiar sounds of the school day, the morning hymn, the recitation of tables, playtime, physical training in the yard in which the voice of the teacher sounded clear and separate like a duck in a distant farmyard. I heard my mother below with the carpet sweeper. She came up with my breakfast at nine, egg and milk at ten, beef tea at eleven and dinner at mid-day. If I wanted her between I pounded on the floor with the metal head, made from a shot-down Zeppelin, of my grandfather's walking stick.

The doctor Harry Dixon was a heavy man with a red face like a pork butcher, whose cross-eyed chauffeur flung open for him in quick succession the door of his car and of the patient's home. The doctor was not treated as a normal tradesman. Women got up in the dark to scour the house the day he was coming. The bed sheets were changed after breakfast and there was no food or drink until after he had been lest marks were made. We were frightened of him. He had the power to sentence people to hospital or even to pronounce their doom but what really alarmed us and what made my mother regress to the servants' deference she had learned as a child was his size, his knowledge, his wealth and a social position of such elevation that he commanded a seat at the front of the main stand at Turf Moor. He came wheezing up the stairs through the smoke of his Turkish cigarette, shook the floorboards of the bedroom with his stride and leaned over me grunting and gasping, his ear lowered to his short rigid stethoscope, so that my whole field of vision was filled with his centre parting and sunburnt pate. He rose and expressed cautious satisfaction that the case was progressing, with the implication that it would require a longish course of treatment. He wrote a prescription, fired off a few affabilities, reloaded his amber cigarette holder and went. We laughed at nothing with relief.

Eric who had been banished from the room when I was first ill himself contracted measles and was brought back. We were as excited as though we had not met for months. It was like a mess when some popular person comes back from a posting or a pub when a regular returns from prison. We made such an uproar the neighbours thumped in protest on the fire back with the poker. His high spirits troubled our mother. He sang in a loud voice. He threw his soft toys at the jugs on the washhand stand. He would not stay under the clothes, which especially distressed her because there was no heat in the bedroom and cold was supposed to turn measles into something more malignant. Often he resumed the day's uproar in his sleep, though our parents spent the evening calming him like people banking down a fire. They would read or tell him stories or sing lulling songs:

> I love little pussy, her coat is so warm
> And if I don't hurt her, she'll do me no harm.
> So I won't pull her tail or drive her away
> And pussy and Eric together will play.

He was enthralled by stories and songs. He would subside into an angelic calm in which one could almost see the pictures of his imagination reflected in his blue eyes. Besides him across the pillow reposed his 'family', Dismal Desmond, a teddy bear, a giraffe with a limp neck and a stuffed bird of bright colours by courtesy of the representative of Kiwi boot polish. Eric kept only the outside strip of the mattress for himself. Sometimes when the stories or the singing ended he would turn his face to the bars and drift off to sleep. But equally he could fling back the bedclothes and rattle about his cot like an ape that has seen the bananas coming. My mother was in tears and my father began to use for the first time the sharp army style of commands that was to become through the years his normal mode of address to us.

Eric's nightmares began after the first hour of sleep. He would stir and sign and groan a little, then shout in a voice tremulous with sorrow and weep. He could not be awakened. Our parents spoke to console and comfort him and wiped away with a flannel the sweat which stood on his forehead and darkened the hair about his neck. Nothing he shouted was understandable. The weeping went through phases of lulls and commotion like a thunderstorm. After ten minutes he would shout less often and sigh as he had at the beginning and of his own accord slide down and sleep. These bouts went on until he was about ten. He did not recall them the next day. No cause was ever identified. They seem to have done him no harm.

At the Co-op branch shoe shop my father managed in Accrington road a clogger and two shoe repairers belted away all day at their lasts, taking nails from their mouths and hammering with rocking rhythms. He took in repairs at the counter and sold occasional pairs of shoes and clogs from the shelves, and he performed on the machines, the stitcher, the finisher with its whirling brushes, and the carborundum wheel whose note climbed to a high pitch when the edge of a sole was brought into contact. From a block away you could hear the machines and the hammering and the deeper roar of an extractor fan set in the wall which showered dirt and leather particles over citizens in Accrington road. When I went in the men looked up and spoke through a mouthful of nails. I could never make out what they said.

One of them, William Breckell, had children of about our age. Our visits to his family were adventures into a different world. They lived 'on t' scheme' and kept a swearing parrot. The scheme was the slum clearance programme under which families were moved to the brick and pebbledash council houses bounded on one side by farms and on the other by Cherry Fold playing fields. The builders were still at work on the estate. Everything smelled of wood and new concrete, but some of the gardens already looked as though they had been cultivated for years. The houses had electricity. At Breckells' we trooped up and down stairs and saw the light switched on in each room. They said there was going to be a bus route which would connect them with Burnley centre and hence with the rest of the world.

We went on weekdays while the menfolk were still at work. The house like most on the scheme was full of children. At tea they all reached and shouted. The older ones assisted, cuffed and pacified the infants. Their granny sitting back in an armchair was attentively consulted and things offered to her in an abundance which it pleased her to deprecate. The parrot said nothing. The meal ended suddenly in an explosion of shouts and crumbs and we swarmed out with bikes and balls across the playing field. Children came from all directions like figures in a Giles cartoon and played in clusters across the green field. I had never seen anything so marvellous. The air smelled of mown grass and builders' sand.

Back at the house one of the daughters was persuaded to give a recital at the piano which I imagined was in some way a part of council house living like switching on electric lights and using the playing fields. They then hospitably bent their efforts to make the parrot swear. 'Daddy's learned him,' they said. We clustered round the cage eager for a mouthful. He was a taciturn bird. They made every effort to induce him, themselves framing blasphemies and obsceni- ties for which Mrs Breckell rebuked them. He gave a brief squawk. They shrieked with shock and delight. 'He swore,' they all shouted, 'he swore.' I was very disappointed. It was clear that William Breckell had taught him with his mouth full of nails. My mother who had been uncomfortable during this part of the evening's entertainment hastily agreed that the parrot had sworn most distinctly. She was easily satisfied. The family walked half way back home with us.

Another home opened to us. My mother's cousin Nellie Battersby and her family had come from Whiston to live close by. Harry Battersby drove a lorry and trailer carrying fruit and vegetables from Liverpool docks to the wholesale market in Leeds. He was faster than the Leeds and Liverpool canal but not much. It was a grinding journey over the lanes of the Pennines, particularly in snow. Burnley was convenient as a mid-way point and because we were there

and auntie Abbie. On a preliminary visit auntie Nellie
reconciled herself to the frightening prospect of the move
from their country village. 'It's not as though we'll be
coming among strangers,' she kept saying. When she went
back letters were exchanged. We ran down the hall to get
them and my mother read them out. When auntie Nellie
wrote in the future tense she, like my grandmother, added
the letters D.V., deo volente, God willing. 'Harry will call
on Wednesday for the keys D.V.' 'Our cat won't go to live
with Mother so we shall have to bring him and hope he will
settle in Burnley D.V.' 'The curtain poles we have here can
be sawn in two and fit the bedrooms there D.V.'

The house they had rented was on Padiham road. My
mother went through the ritual of scrubbing it out from top
to bottom. When we arrived with our buckets and mops it
was still damp and tide-marked from the scrubbing its
previous tenants had given it on departure. It had to be
done again. You never know who'd been there; they might
not have been too particular. But if you did and they were,
the scrubbing still had to be done. It was a part of the
ceremony of moving house which it was our duty to
observe. My mother put plenty of disinfectant in the water
just as a priest, anxious to do especially well in another
parish, might heap an extra helping of incense on the censer.

My grandfather arrived. He came through the echoing
rooms, briefly observed that my mother on her hands and
knees was doing the scrubbing thoroughly, and went out to
inspect the yard and make himself known to the neighbours.
He wore as usual his bowler hat and starched front. His
contribution on these occasions was strictly social and administrative. He enjoyed arranging to get the gas turned on
and engaging grandly and without authority such passing
tradesmen as caught his approval. A tin of pea-green paint
found in the coal house tempted him for once to manual
work. He slapped it on everywhere. It never set. Several of
the windows were sealed for ever. The Battersbys themselves became adept at flitting past sticky doors. Some of
their visitors stuck like flies.

On the day they were to arrive fires were lighted throughout the house, downstairs and also in the grates of the

bedrooms where they were kindled for only two of life's occasions, the arrival as now of new tenants and the departure from this world of old ones. The damp soot of the chimneys warmed. The rooms smelt as acrid as gun turrets. Steam rose from the newly-scrubbed boards and condensed on the unopenable windows. The warmth of the welcome brought tears to auntie Nellie's eyes.

The lorry came earlier than we expected. We heard the brakes and there it was at the edge of the pavement, its sidelights gleaming at the front of a towering load of furniture. Our new relatives grinned from the cab. Harry Battersby jumped down and came round. Irene, pink and blond and four years old, was passed down sleeping, then Leslie a shy boy a little older than myself, then auntie Nellie. She made a dumpy descent imperilled by advice, encouragement and assistance offered in greater measure than she could acknowledge or cope with. Uncle Harry captured the cat with a fist like a boxing glove and my grandfather carried it through the house by the scruff and pitched it into the coal shed with a harsh reproof as though it had deliberately done something to disrupt the reception. Uncle Harry, assisted by uncle Ben and my father, began to hump in the furniture. They were all good at handling things and glad to get the women and children out of the way so they could enjoy the rhythm of the job. We went to our house for a meal. My grandfather who had been carrying in hearth brushes and plant pots stayed on for a while to supervise then came and joined us. He detailed to auntie Nellie the trades and services he had engaged on her behalf. She was a nervous woman and effusively grateful but one of her many apprehensions was the cost of living in a town and as his recital ended the cake remained uneaten on her plate. She addressed him as 'uncle Ted' which clapped a new identity on him as though somebody had given him a false nose. But this was a formal occasion, he was on his dignity, he refused to catch my eye.

Harry Battersby had been a coal miner in Wigan before he took to the wheel. He looked like the heroes of stories in the Adventure and the Rover with bristling hair, a low forehead and a heavy jaw. He was always in a good humour.

On Friday nights he brought home deep stiff paper bags full of fruit and nuts which the company sold cheap to employees. Evidently it was not yet the practice of drivers to knock off what they wanted. Uncle Harry set out the fruit and nuts on the table in the form of the figures of a clock. We spun a knife and won whatever the blade pointed at when it stopped. Eric and Irene as learners had first to say what the time would be if the blade was the hour hand. Uncle Harry asked us riddles and sometimes recited poems in the form of a riddle:

If a feller met a feller in a field of fitches
Could a feller tell a feller if his belly itches?

I did not know for years what fitches were until I discovered that it was the dialect word for a field plant known as the vetch. But the rhyme stuck, no doubt because of my mother's anxiety to discourage me from repeating it. She said it wasn't nice but uncle Harry was very good hearted.

He was a supporter of the Labour party and a reader of the Daily Herald. I later gathered that the ends he had in mind were similar to uncle Frank's but he spoke of them seldom and humourously and hoped for their achievement without blowing people up and reducing his mother to tears. He had faith in the Daily Herald and it was a nasty blow when it was shattered. Something he knew of at first hand was the subject of a report which was inaccurate and misleading. There was no accounting for it. He was shocked and bewildered. 'How do they expect us to get more intelligent,' he asked, 'when they print lies in th' Herald?'

He was good at blow football. His blast hit you at the other end of the table like a gale coming off the sea and the ball struck your goalie with such force that he spun round and round on his horizontal support. These goalies, pressed-tin cut-outs, bothered me. They wore cricket caps, and long johns, and striped jerseys like outfield players, and they had handlebar moustaches. Their style was fifty years out of date. It was also subversive. It weakened my pleas for a proper pair of football boots when it could be pointed out that I already had a nice pair of hobnailed clompers as worn by the tin blow football goalies.

Auntie Nellie was a jelly of a woman, awobble with trepidation. Her abiding fear was of road traffic. There were still only a million motor vehicles in the whole of Britain but auntie Nellie, coming from the country, seemed to believe most of them thundered along Padiham road. It was not in fact their number that was to be feared but, as I have said earlier, their alarming ability to home in on pedestrians. Now in 1930 an open season was declared by the abolition of the 20 m.p.h. speed limit. Motorists dispatched 30,000 pedestrians before the government four years later saw fit to call a halt with the introduction of a speed limit of 30 miles an hour in built-up areas. Auntie Nellie was not alone in standing poised with her brood on the pavement edge and fluttering across like a hen that has seen a fox.

Leslie was a country boy, quiet and slow-spoken. He went bird-nesting alone and to my amazement played neither cricket nor football. Although older he was in my class at school and did not do well, which was a handicap to him when we went round with the muck cart competing for marbles brought up from the street grates. The horse stopped at the grates without bidding and the man dredged up the sludge with a long-handled scoop. He allowed the surplus water to run back and paddled his fingers in the sludge. Sometimes a marble was revealed, like a nugget in a miner's pan. He then asked us questions – riddles, multiplications, the names of colonies and dominions – and the first to answer correctly got the marble. Sometimes he did not put the question to the clamour of free competition but singled out a boy who had not yet won and asked him an easy one. Leslie was singled out and went home with his marble. Auntie Nellie was proud of him but was then struck by the danger from the cloud of germs that must be released from the stirred up sludge. An education and even a collection of marbles would not be adequate compensation for landing up in the fever hospital or the cemetery.

One day Leslie came and made rigid a wilting crane I had constructed with Meccano. The result was impressive but even more so the sureness of his work, the patient analysis of faults, the dismantling and the spreading out in order of required parts, the handling of screwdriver and spanner. It was skill quite beyond my command. It brought me to sober terms with my abilities. I knew that I did well at muck-cart marbles because brighter children in the class, mainly girls, were not present to compete. I could not remotely match my cousin Stanley in his perception of the modes and motives of adults, in the weight of his knowledge or in his artistic talent which had turned their living room into a one-man exhibition. I was passed over for a speaking part in the next Sunday school performance and left among the skippers. Even my mother came to accept that my early success in naming some of the animals on the alphabetical building blocks had been a false dawn. All I could do well was to kick a football at goals chalked on the street side of the brick school wall. Even that came from practice rather than talent: I kept at it when relays of boys went home tired or bored. It began to dawn on me that a kind of donkey engine persistence would have to serve for a shortfall of talent.

I come last in the Battersby family to the preposterous Irene. By the age of four she had cultivated an individual laugh. She stood pink and chubby in the corner and snuffled and snorted. Auntie Nellie rounded on her. 'What are you laughing at, you great daft thing?' She threatened to give her a good hiding and put her out. Silence. Then the chortling started again. More threats. Another silence, in which the rest of us tried unsuccessfully to concentrate on something other than waiting for the next outburst. I began to notice in auntie Nellie's rebuke 'What are you laughing at?' a puzzlement not wholly genuine. In threatening Irene she glanced at me to be sure I noticed. She even apologised to me directly for Irene's behaviour. It sank in at last that everybody knew what Irene was laughing at. She was laughing at me. I was amazed. In what way was I laughable? Even to ask the question is to succumb to the persecution. It put me off my stroke completely. I turned up my scowl to maximum. It had intimidated quite a few boys but only provoked Irene to such a crescendo of chortling and snuffling that auntie Nellie did at last put her out. It had not occurred to me before that I was ludicrous. I did not know how to cope with it. I gave Irene a wide berth and watched with paranoid suspicion any welcoming smiles from girls lest they should of a sudden explode into mocking laughter.

One Sunday we turned out from the chapel in procession. The banner was carried by colliers in their·best suits who when the brass band struck up put out their cigarettes in a shower of sparks. Those of us who had them wore page boy suits. Girls carried baskets of flowers. Policemen kept step. Jesus smiled down from the banner borne along beneath the tramway cables. More bands, banners and processions converged from side streets. All the Sunday schools in Burnley, in England, and indeed in the whole world, we were told, had taken to the streets this day in commemoration of Robert Raikes, the founder 150 years previously of Sunday schools. 'Sabbath schools are England's glory,' we sang. I do not remember where we marched to, but it was a long way. 'Sunday scholars should be thankful,' we sang, 'for the blessings they enjoy'. We were glad to get back and sit down. We were given coffee which we never got at any other time and a currant bun offered from a large wooden tray. We had already been given medals bearing an effigy of Robert Raikes. We could see what they meant about being thankful. On the other hand we felt we had been sold short in the lesson on Mr Raikes which preceded the procession. In particular we had been denied details of the behaviour of the children personally tutored by him which he described as 'so horrid as to convey to the serious mind an idea of hell rather than any other place'. What, we asked agog, did they actually do? The answers were evasive, thin and unconvincing: Sabbath-breaking (which meant buying ice cream on Sundays), gambling and wagering (what was the difference and what with?) and swearing (everybody did and even parrots tried). We gathered that we were not going to be told. The 'streets of his native Gloucester', which were identified as the place where children fell into unspeakable sinfulness, took on for us the fascination of the Cities of the Plain. But wickedness, it seemed, did not prevail. The good Raikes tanned it out of them. In his work of 'botanising in human nature', the text of the lesson said, 'he found he could not dispense with the birching stool'.

That was the founder of the Sunday school. The founder of the church John Wesley advocated much the same approach to children:

> Break their wills betimes; begin this great work before they can run alone, before they can speak plain or perhaps speak at all. Let him have nothing he cries for, absolutely nothing, great or small. Make him do as he is bid, if you whip him ten times running to effect it. Break his will now and his soul will live and he will probably bless you to all eternity.

The influence of the godly men had long passed in my time. Our Sunday school was a wholly benevolent place, run by teachers who were more ordinary and usually a bit older than day school teachers. They did the job because they were fond of children and measured their success by the children's happiness. The primary department was bright with welcome and assurance. Here was Jesus who told good stories, raised the dead, multiplied fishes, made the blind to see, walked on water and would gladly sort out anybody on request. We believed in the benevolence of Jesus because of the kindness of the teachers. We believed we had a place in the sight of God because they remembered our names. It was a safe world, generous, open, unexacting, and sometimes, rarely enough to be memorable, we caught a glimpse of the majesty of the Christian centuries and the stirring excitement of men when Christ was amongst them. The spell would pass but for the present it made of no account the mean kind of game in which at day school we were shuffled to a different seat according to how well we answered arithmetical questions on a neatly torn scrap of paper. Sunday school helped us to recognize the trivial for what it was. It also taught us to count our blessings. The greatest asset in my life was to know early that I was lucky.

10 · SUMMER OF THE AVIATORS

The summer of 1930 was hot. Tar and creosote bubbled on the shacks and fences of the hen pens, the pools in the cinder street dried up and baked, frogs came into the coal place, old men sat all day packed on park benches like racks of biscuits in an oven. We travelled. At Easter my grandparents took me to St Helens to stay with their friend, Mrs Corbett. We accomplished the journey of about thirty miles in four stages, three Ribble motor buses, to Blackburn, to Wigan, to St Helens and then the local tram. My grandmother wrote a card home to say we had had a good journey and arrived safely. Tomorrow we hoped to go to New Brighton D.V.

We all felt guilty about leaving behind my brother Eric, too young at three to come on this kind of holiday but smart enough to have seen through the stratagem by which we intended to sneak off while he was having his afternoon nap. He howled. Our mother and grandparents attempted to console and bribe him. They ran an auction of future compensations bidding up with increasing recklessness as bus time approached. He amassed a credit of what amounted to a season ticket at Lowerhouse cricket club, ten pounds of sweets, a trip to the end of the Amazon and lifelong exemption from wearing white sandals. In the end we grabbed our luggage and ran. His distress remained with us through the journey. We hardly spoke. I think we all wished we had not come.

Mrs Corbett was a handsome woman with a finely structured face and upswept white hair. She moved briskly and gracefully in long dresses. The house, in Windleshaw road, was sweet with the smell of fruit and plants. First thing in the morning she gathered the plants in armfuls and carried them into the yard for watering. I was given to understand then or later that the plants were solace to her for a hard life. In youth she had been in domestic service along with my grandmother, having left home and the post of an untrained school teacher because of unhappiness caused by her father's second marriage. She became engaged to Jim Corbett, wholesale and retail greengrocer, boon companion and merry tippler, who improved permitted visits to the kitchen where she was employed as a cook by excursions into the wine cellar. He became persona non grata to the house, then through the years in the sad way of drunks to everybody else, business friends, cronies and finally family. When he died it was a relief. Her job of running a business and bringing up a family was fairly plain sailing once he was gone.

Mrs Corbett's son Ralph in time took on the wholesale greengrocery business, a shy rubicund man who possessed two motor vehicles, a lorry in which we did trips in the early morning to the docks at Liverpool or to farms on the sandy plain round Ormskirk, and his first motor car. His mother treated him as a coachman, calling out instructions and admonitions from the back seat and in a slightly lower voice talking about him as though he were not there. 'Not so fast, Ralph. Slow down. He's doing quite well but they spend too much on the children. Proceed ahead, Ralph. I've changed my mind about visiting Rainford today. He doesn't do well at market. He was always slow at arithmetic and now he's left counting on his fingers while the mentally more spry make off with the bargains. Keep your eyes on the road, Ralph. Ted can see the crops for himself. He ran over a hen last week. It may not be a hen next time, Ralph. Change gear. I can't talk to Maggie over this noise.'

Her younger son Will had a position at Pilkingtons. I do not know what the position was but it was something better than blowing glass or humping panes about. He wore a suit with a watch chain across his waistcoat. He had fastidious habits. Before his meal he gargled at the gully in the yard, and back inside scrubbed his nails so vigorously that the window became opaque with splattered soap. I gathered that he indulged in these eccentricities because he was a bachelor.

To be a bachelor did not mean merely that a young man was unmarried but carried the connotation that marriage had passed him by. He might be known to have had 'a disappointment', an engagement to marry having been broken off, which was a matter of graver concern then than the breakdown of a marriage now. Engagements commonly lasted six years in which savings were accumulated and household objects assembled and patterns set of visits to relatives. Holidays might be taken together but usually in the company of another couple or delegates from either family or both. Sexual opportunities must have been few and furtive. Patience and restraint were enjoined. Pregnancy was dreaded as some people now dread the Bomb, and one can see why. Few families could earn more than their keep. A household begun without some essential furniture and some small savings would be bare for many years. They could never hope to catch up. But the horror of premature pregnancy was out of proportion to its mere economic consequences. It was shameful, an affliction on a family as painful as bereavement. Mothers turned grey overnight, fathers and brothers threatened violence. Young men transformed at a doctor's word from suitors into villains became, according to temperament, sheepish pram-pushers or intrepid emigrants eager to pursue their fortune in the empire overseas.

I suppose many of these long engagements proceeded relentlessly to marriage long after the contracting parties were bored with each other and disenchanted with their prospects together. Escape was more costly to a woman. Because of the length of engagement and the convention which placed it between the ages of 20 and 26, once she had reached the half-way point it would seem too late to start again. It was like long flights over the Pole or the Pacific. The half-way point was also the point of no return. There was also a stigma on a woman whose engagement had been broken. She was handled goods, secondhand. There was a moral taint.

So 'disappointments' were spoken of in hushed voices, with understanding and the judgment of making no judgment. Will Corbett had been engaged to a young lady with bobbed hair whose photographs lay on the table when I came into the room. Mrs Corbett collected them together and put them in a box. She said something quietly to my grandparents by way of summing up which sounded to mean that the young lady's health was uncertain or perhaps that she was not quite compos mentis. It was a matter for pity and for the sadness that surrounds people who exist now only in the past. They observed a silence, then struck a cheerful note.

I went to play football with Ralph's son Cyril and his friends who apologised for the roundness of their ball and then persisted in running up and down with it tucked under their arm. My grandfather explained that it was a different code. We went to see it practised professionally by St Helens Recs. Bruisers formed themselves into heaps and steamed. It was shocking to hear it called football. Some years later I knew a youth who went to the home of his girl friend in South Lancashire where they hearkened to the Rugby League results then turned the wireless off when the soccer results were about to begin. His father was astounded to hear of such malpractice and gravely counselled him to extricate himself. 'You don't want to get mixed up with that class of folk.'

My grandfather who was more liberal and a hedonist grasped at such pleasures as might be enjoyed, the fleetness of the players when eventually they were allowed to get up, the condition of the sward and the pleasantness of the afternoon. He ingratiated us to our neighbours on the terraces by seeking instruction in the game. It had already been explained to me that Mrs Corbett was an Anglican and a Tory but nevertheless a good woman. It was now apparent that those who watched Rugby League were also to be approved of, and this exploding universe of tolerance was due to be further expanded the following day to include the Welsh. We were to sail to Llandudno in a steamer with a

yellow funnel which we had seen at anchor at Liverpool. It
rained and we did not go. Drops like tears ran down the
window pane. I grieved for Wales. In my grandfather's
telling it was among the most enchanting of foreign lands.
And indeed it is, though I did not discover that in his time.

The summer was so hot that the caretaker was sent round to
force open windows stuck with paint since the school was
built. The breeze came in, raising papers and carrying the
choruses of tables and verses chanted in other classrooms.
Girls wore print frocks. Boys suffered under the weight of
flannel shirts, serge blazers and trousers down to the tops of
our socks. A woollen vest was deemed necessary at all
seasons as a protection against catching cold. My grandmother who was upholstered like a sofa would quote, 'Cast
not a clout till May is out.' Clout to us did not mean a
garment but in the dialect a blow. She could not understand
our mirth or the charades of assault and battery set off by
this sensible saw. Flies abounded. Their hum in the grocers'
shops rose above the chatter and the note of the bacon slicer.
Fly papers hung everywhere black with insects but still
capable of sticking to your hair. Children had pale patches
on their skulls where the hair and glue and flies had been cut
out. Smaller ones stuck themselves up with tar poked from
between the cobbles of the road.

We were grubby all the time, covered by a patina of soot
from the atmosphere which on hot days ran in streaks. We
had a bath once a week on Friday nights, preceded by a
hair-washing in which we enjoyed the pleasure of nodding
soot blobs on to the porcelain of the washbasin. We had a
good wash which included knees and neck and ears morning
and night and a swill at midday. Workers washed and
changed immediately on returning home. To be caught
'sitting in your muck' was scandalous. We had a clean shirt
once a week. Top clothes of flannel and serge could not be
washed and were never cleaned. I do not know whether
there were any dry cleaners. Friction burnished the elbows
and the seats of trousers, creating an ebony surface from the
ingrained soot. Through the years the suits of old men were
transformed over their whole surface into some sort of shiny

carboniferous compound. From a distance they looked to
have been struck in tarmac. Dirt in the eyes was a daily pain
in summer.

The breezes of 1930 brought intimations of a wider world.
Sounds carried in the still heat: above the cluck of the hen
pens and the hum of the mills we would hear a distant farm
dog and a mowing machine and trains. We heard the small
brave snarl of an engine up in the sky, and we instantly
knew what it would be. We flocked to the window of the
classroom. A small biplane with a snub nose was riding the
warm upcurrents at the side of a puff of cumulus cloud.
Everybody knew about 'aeros' because for most of May a
lengthening red ribbon on a wall map had marked the
zigzag stages of Amy Johnson's solo flight to Australia. The
aeroplane was the first most of us had seen.

It was a year of heavy blossom. On Sunday afternoons
we struck further afield. We called our walks exploring. I
read about the distant lands of the empire in my father's
Sunday school prize books. We sang in school a song which
still brings back the heat of that summer and the promise of
foreign shores:

> A sailor boy I met one day, singing yo-ho, yo-ho,
> Said he, my ship lies in the dip,
> And waits for the breeze to blow, you know,
> And waits for the breeze to blow.
> O, come with me across the sea
> For there are wonderful sights to see.
> O, come with me across the sea,
> I want you to come with me.

Shortly after Amy Johnson's red ribbon reached Darwin I
learned that we too were going to make a journey of epic
length, to a place so distant that my mother had never
travelled so far and my father not since he returned from the
war. It sounded like another country, a place without
chimneys and tramcars, of flat fields under a towering sky
where even on the hottest days a breeze off the sea rippled
the grass and cooled the haymakers. Great horses pulled the
hay carts and at the end of each row the men and women
with rakes and pikes refreshed themselves from a barrel of

beer or a pitcher of lemonade which kept them slaked and cheerful through the long day. The place was Norfolk. The people we were to stay with were my father's aunt Agnes and her husband Hugh Watson who farmed at Walpole Cross Keys in the Fens.

For our part it was a once and for all grand spree funded by the sale of my father's motor bike. How he persuaded my mother to blue in all the money on one week I do not know. He would certainly not have succeeded if she had had any inkling of the stringency that lay ahead. We all had new clothes. Eric had cream sandals and a white jersey with coloured chickens embroidered round the hem which he was assured would make him at one with the rustic throng. We bought a new trunk reinforced on the outside with two steel bands, strong enough to withstand a lifetime of voyages to India. We went into town and bought three different lots of sweets for the journey.

The whole of a cotton town went on holiday in the same week. Dates between the end of June and September were set by the cotton manufacturers when holidays first began and ritually confirmed in Manchester each year. The wakes week, as it was called in other places, was no less the unalienable property of a town than its town hall and public parks. In Burnley it was known as the Fair Week in honour of the travelling fair which set up on the cattle market for the entertainment of those who stayed at home.

The rest started early, grey figures before dawn, bent under the weight of trunks and suitcases. In the tram with its lights still on children sat drunk with sleep. The station was thronged. Queues at the booking office stretched back under the street lights, the wooden staircases rumbled like a football stand, the platform was so packed there seemed no hope of getting on the train. But we were not going with the rest to Blackpool. Their trains came and went, excursion trains, old engines with only six wheels, and old carriages, gas-lit and upholstered in horse hair. We took the regular train to Manchester. Dawn broke over Bolton.

I cannot remember how often we changed trains or how many companies' lines we travelled on. To cross England from Lancashire to Norfolk is still among the world's

mammoth railway journeys. Chinley up in the Derbyshire
Pennines was one place we changed. In fact we changed
there twice. We had just climbed into one train when we
spotted a porter making off with our new trunk to another
standing at the opposite platform. My father got out and
asked questions. He was by no means convinced but our
new trunk by then had gone into the guard's van and we
had no choice unless we were to lose it but to take our
chance in the dubious train. We had the feeling of travelling
backwards in the wrong direction. I imagined landing after
all at Blackpool but hours after the people from the excursion
trains had claimed the best places on the sands. In our
anxiety we downed the whole consignment of sugared
almonds. Then my father took a sighting on the sun and
announced that we were going in the right direction. We
ran out of the hills, into the wooded farmland of Not-
tinghamshire and on into the Fens, past windmills and
hump-backed bridges, past villages with squat steeples visible from miles away, over level-crossings where rustics
clustered with bicycles, and alongside the shimmering drain-
age ditches which seen on a map or from the air hold the
countryside in a net of waterways. It was evening when we
arrived.

My father's uncle Hugh looked like a farmer in a picture
book. The poor farmers I had visited with my grandfather
on the hills above Bacup were dressed as drab as the moors.
Uncle Hugh was not poor. He was rigged out in tweeds
and changed his hat or cap to suit the occasion two or three
times a day. He had an old English sheepdog instead of a
collie and, far from cursing unsparing efforts, he chuckled at
its failure to round up the fat sheep in the meadow. He had
a stick and a pipe and bowled round in a little motor car.
His three sons worked for him, several labourers, and now
in the strawberry-gathering season all the women from miles
around. They crept over the black earth filling baskets which
were stacked up besides the bicycles at the field gate. A
record was kept by an ancient man for whom a kitchen
chair had been brought out. I was astonished to learn that
the pickers were pemitted to eat all the strawberries they
wished but that a surfeit in early youth had put them off for

life. The strawberries went for jam at a factory at Kings
Lynn. It was the only time that the goods yard at the
wayside station was put to use. Its lines were rusty and the
sleepers grown over with willow herb. An engine came
every day for the vans and stood towering above the signal
box and hissing out steam.

Eric was buckled into his cream sandals and walked
straight out into cow muck. When he had been hosed down
he toppled from a wall into a forest of nettles. I was charged
by a ram. I was put on a horse's back. I had my picture
taken with the sheepdog. My father worked high on a stack,
forking hay about with uncle Hugh's sons. Small yokels in
big caps and cut-down clothes collected at the gate to guffaw
at our speech. We ate at a big table in a room as hot as an
oven. We slept in an attic with a dormer window fitted
with chintz curtains. Outside, high on its gantry was a
water storage tank, and beyond that the goods yard still and
quiet in the early morning and beyond that a great expanse
of country in which you could see the shelter belts and
steeples of distant villages.

Uncle Hugh owned tracts of land beyond the horizon
which we visited in his motor car. He sat at the wheel
squeezed between my father and the door, both of them
with their eyes screwed against the draught and dust that
came through the opened windscreen. Eric and I and Hugh's
son Ernest sat behind in a dickie seat, a bench fitted across
the inside of a sort of boot lid hinged at the bottom. In the
light of what is now known about the aerodynamics of car
shapes we must have been far gone in carbon monoxide
poisoning from the exhaust. At each stop uncle Hugh spoke
briefly of his ambition to leave a farm to each of his sons
and my father briefly expressed admiration of the project.
Both were men of few words.

The places all looked much the same, approached by
straight roads along which the telegraph poles sprouted at
angles. Then we left the ditches and the strawberry fields
and ran into lusher country. We turned into a large field
which I recognised from my father's description, a great
meadow where Suffolk horses strained at haycarts and the
lines of people raked with little progress towards the barrel

of everlasting ale. I noticed a profusion of wild flowers which he had left out of his description, poppies and buttercups and purple thistles by the fence, and great white cumulus clouds against the blue of the sky. It was as though a pencil drawing had blossomed into colour and sprung to life. There was another element he had not mentioned. Aeroplanes rocked about the field and rose into the sky. Uncle Hugh said he let the field to the Air Force but he still had the hay off it. He chuckled as though he thought it a shrewd deal. The taxying aeroplanes passed so close we caught the smell of them, petrol, vegetable oil and the pear-drop aroma of the dope with which their fabric surfaces were smoothed. They bumped past on solid wheels. The ailerons waddled a little, the rudder flapped, the pilot goggled past the struts and through the disc of the whirling propellor. When they turned, the tall grass bent in their slipstream like an unfolding fan. They whined down the cricket pitch of a runway, rose wobbling a little, climbed, banked into a turn and hurtled back on the downwind leg. The Suffolk horses and the Norfolk haymakers took no notice. To me the scene was not only unexpected but until then unimaginable, yet at the same time it seemed known and familiar. I felt I had been there before and I knew I should return.

We went to Hunstanton where the tide comes in fast across the flat sands. We went to somewhere on the Wash in the hope that we might be able to lay hands on King John's jewels. We went to market at Sutton Bridge where in the company of friends uncle Hugh's sing-song became completely incomprehensible. They took no notice of the beasts in the ring but laughed together like a jolly heap of turnips. Eric had a bilious attack. We made an expedition of elaborately concealed purpose; on our return our hosts were good enough to pretend to be astonished to be given presents. The visit was of only six days but the memories have endured more vividly than those of some years. I remember the feeling of loss in Claremont Sunday school on the day after we returned. The sun, coming from behind a cloud, brightened a frosted window with blank light. I was grieved by the empty prospect of days and months remote from the fens of Norfolk. My father promised we should go again next year. A year seemed an unattainable time. And then we did not go. I did not return to that part of the country until I went to Cranwell.

11 · A NEW NEIGHBOURHOOD

The Sunday at the end of Burnley Fair Week was always a still day. The town lay quiet as though it had been abandoned to an enemy who had not yet arrived. The soot had settled. The sky was blue for the only time in the year. Irridescent patches of oil formed at the loading bays on the canal.

The place came to life on the Monday morning like somebody late for work. Doors banged, clogs clattered, tramcars ran, the oiled pistons and flywheels of the great mill engines moved again, buzzers sounded, railway sidings panted and clanked, the wheels of the pithead winding gear turned, a hundred mill chimneys smoked. No one returning from holiday in the summer of 1930 would have seen them as the smokestacks of a sinking fleet nor have understood that the recession was not a passing shadow but the onset of evening in the empire on which the sun never set.

Cotton was the first industry of the Industrial Revolution. By 1914 it employed directly or indirectly a million people. It was by far Britain's biggest export and brought in a quarter of all overseas earnings. The mill towns divided the world between them. Blackburn wove for India, Burnley for China. Blackburn looms were wider than Burnley looms because Indians cocooned themselves in cloth whereas the Chinese were content with a shirt. The idea that foreigners, 'natives', might some day start to roll their own had been thought ludicrous. But they did, with newer machinery or cheaper labour or both. By the time the need sank in for reorganisation and re-equipment in Lancashire it was too late. The trade had gone. In India, once the biggest market, resistance to British cotton was elevated to a political and spiritual principle. In 1931 they got Gandhi to come to Blackburn to see the damage he was causing by egging people on to weave their own dhotis. It must have been a mutually incomprehensible conversation. At all events the saintly man was rubbed up the wrong way and went home more disobliging than when he came. He confirmed his boycott on English cotton. Seventy-four mills in Blackburn closed in the next four years. Imported cotton goods, from Japan and Hong Kong, began to compete in the British home market. Mills went on short time. Towns which had been among the most prosperous in the world sank into poverty.

Shortly after we got back from Norfolk my father's job as a Co-op branch manager finished. People short of money were reverting to clogs. The branch shops would be kept open for clogging. All shoe repairs would be centralized in a factory. My father was given a job there as a machinist. He hid from us whatever disappointment he may have felt. The reorganisation was sensible, and he may have counted himself fortunate still to have a job when most of the shoe repairers at the branch shops had been put on the dole. At any rate we moved house to Hinton street near his new work as though a new and exciting adventure was beginning. Harry Battersby piled our stuff on his lorry, uncle Ben helped to hump it off, auntie Nellie assisted at the ritual scrubbing of the old house and auntie Abbie at the new. Grandfather Sephton turned up in his bowler hat to attend to the social and administrative aspects of the move. He was kept away from the paint.

Hinton street was the better type of terraced house fronted by a strip of garden eighteen inches wide in which privet sprouted. One of the two upstairs rooms had been partitioned to make a bathroom. The house was smaller than Lionel street but situated at the very centre of the universe. Everywhere that mattered lay within a quarter of a mile – Turf Moor football and cricket grounds, the home of our cousins the Kerrys, the Pentridge pictures, and only fifty yards away at the end of our street the open space of Fulledge recreation ground, and beyond that the river and the parkland of Towneley and beyond again the hills of the Todmorden valley where the snow often remained on north faces until April. It was a good place for children.

The Co-op factories stretched into the fields, low buildings of new stone which if they had had no chimney would have looked more like a school. Because we had only the recreation ground to cross Eric and I were allowed to go alone to meet our father coming out of work. We passed the base of the chimney. Once we stood back and looked up it. Never again; the ornamental top seemed to be reeling over as though it was beginning to topple. My father warmed our hands in his in the pockets of his overcoat. We asked him what might happen if the chimney fell over. He said it wouldn't. He had no fears of his own that I ever detected and no awareness of the fears of others.

Fulledge chapel and school were sooty buildings three storeys high on opposite sides of a cobbled yard. A shelter and a high wall completed the enclosure. You could smell the lavatories from a hundred yards away. The desks were of the type where half a dozen children sit along a plank at a working top held horizontal by iron clamps at the end. Elsewhere they had been superceded and sold to the cricket club where the clamps were released so the top became the seat back. The bannisters were studded with conical brass buttons to prevent sliding or at least to make it painful. The high windows resonated to the banging of water pipes of a gauge to suit a battleship but incapable of heating the rooms.

It had been a Wesleyan day school. When the council took it over they seem to have got the original staff thrown in with the desks and the buildings. Ancient women crossed the cobbles, the teachers of the lower classes who had so put the wind up my cousin Stanley that his parents had him transferred to another school. I missed their tuition, being old enough to go straight to the top class conducted by Miss Lancaster. She was of an intermediate time, not a crone but not either of the new generation of young teachers. She had grey hair and horn-rimmed spectacles, wore tweeds and earned her pay. The class, isolated in a large room at the top of the building, was in her sole charge. We did not go to the school's morning assembly. We had our own. She sat at the piano and banged out the hymns. She taught from bell to bell and she taught everybody. She was never unfair. She never held up anybody to ridicule. Nobody liked her.

Every morning she wrote ten spellings on the blackboard. We sang out in unison the letters and the word, giving special attention to unphonetic syllables underlined in red so that nobody when the board was twirled over would have an excuse for spelling the ending of portmanteau in the same way as potato. She responded in no way to pupils who when required to write the words tried to drum up recollection by breathing in gasps or rattling the stem of their pen against their teeth. But neither did she chide us for getting spellings wrong. We simply had them added to the next day's quota, much as my mother as a child got what she had left at one meal served with the next.

Miss Lancaster had a cane which was a symbol of authority rather than a weapon, not the sort intended to be whirled round the head but a short baton that might have served a bandmaster. When I held out my right hand with a bandaged thumb she demanded the left and remarked 'We don't cane sore thumbs here'. It must have been an off day. Normally she did not stoop to moralising. The cane upset her judgment, perhaps because it was superfluous. Her authority did not need its support. It was an old cane, cut down perhaps from some bruising instrument shattered long ago on somebody's backside and abandoned by the Wesleyans when they evacuated the day school. Miss Lancaster did not know not to cane girls. With boys there was an understood convention. She showed no animosity and they showed no defiance. She rapped their hand. They went back to their desk pretending to feel no pain. Girls were unpredictable and a caning could be upsetting like a bungled execution. They would withdraw their hand at the last moment. In grabbing them by the wrist she sometimes wrenched their arm and shoulder. They would nurse the smitten hand between their thighs and rock and weep. Some went back with a smile and burst into tears half an hour later. It was embarrassing and shameful.

I had a struggle with mental arithmetic which I had not even heard of. I called it 'medicine' and thus started a train of observations in a secret dossier compiled by school teachers which led to the conclusion that I was deaf and eventually helped to put me in hospital for a tonsils and adenoids operation. But arithmetic of any sort was preferable to literature. Poetry was the most painful, so mawkish that you could not look anybody in the face. Cruel parents chivvied boys to repeat for the company verses they had learned at school.

> I've got a pair of nice new laces,
> Knickerbockers and a pair of braces.

Where had the bard lived and when? This was 1931. Only Bernard Shaw still wore knickerbockers, making a fool of himself in the Soviet Union. Who would care about laces? Who would boast about new braces? Poetry came in two styles. One was of false sentiments aimed at schooling children in piety and docility and, as above, enthusiastic gratitude for the kind of things that came up with the ration; the other was of simpering fancies clothed in 'poetic' words churned out by an underworld of old ladies with cats and potty parsons.

Prose was served up in the late afternoon like a helping of suet pudding at the end of a meal. The 'readers' were lifted out of a wooden chest, books so old that their title was barely legible but carefully repaired with linen on the spine and sticky paper no longer quite transparent on torn pages. The ink had turned brown on the names past generations of children had inscribed and on the sentences they formed from the heading, Contents: Cows Ought Not To Eat Nasty Turnip Stalks. This was the brightest sentence in the book. The text was a stodge of extracts ground out by Victorian hacks paid by weight and volume. Descriptions went on for pages. Encounters were reduced to reflections. Nobody did anything. There was no story, which was tedious to us because, unlike the Victorian pupils, we knew better things. Stories in the Beano and Comic Cuts romped along. Motion pictures moved.

We formed our desks into a square and the chief monitor read first, Arthur Wilkinson, a ruddy boy with a watered quiff who smelled of his corduroy trousers. He was a good sergeant, calm, efficient and impersonal. He was also a good reader, capable of controlling his breath through sentences of Proustian length and complexity. His was the top group and I had been placed in it because of a false deduction drawn from my turning up in boots instead of clogs. The dossier which from my earliest school days branded me as a 'backward reader' had still to arrive. Even without it Miss Lancaster had me spotted from the other side of the room the moment I opened my mouth. She raised her head like a gun dog, then without fuss demoted me to the second group and the next day to the third. I tumbled down the divisions like a football team gone to pot. One reason why I was so badly outshone was that we did not resume where we left off but went back a couple of pages and the best readers read first. They squelched through a familiar part of the bog of words whereas the less able of us had to face uncharted waters. This going back day after day was a final heaping on of tedium. It was like the labours of Sisyphus or playing snakes and ladders on a board wickedly designed to prevent any player from ever reaching home. Nobody had ever got to the end of the book. The earlier pages were grubby and ink-stained and mottled with age, the last pages fresh as when they left the press sixty years before.

Normal lessons were the best part of the day. We disliked the poetry and the reading. The hymns we sang in the morning were even worse, bleak with the vision of eternity in a vast echoing hall.

> Holy, holy, holy! all the saints adore Thee,
> Casting down their golden crowns around the glassy sea;
> Cherubim and seraphim falling down before Thee,
> Which were and art and evermore shall be.

We sang it every morning. The last verse ends:

> God in three persons, blessed Trinity.

A funny choice. It was not even as though there were many among us likely to profit from a grounding in Hebrew or theology. The feeling of the hymn must have been agreeable to Miss Lancaster. Did she understand it? She never explained the words, though she was usually meticulous about meanings. I suspect she thought of verse exactly as we did, rhetoric in a specialized vocabulary from which no sensible meaning could be derived.

There is one more thing to be said about Miss Lancaster's class. Pupils left it more able and confident than when they arrived. Lessons sprang from her coldness which might not have been learned any other way. She seldom praised or blamed and thereby she freed work from a burden of emotion. It was an end in itself, not done as a means of currying favour or avoiding displeasure. What had to be learned had to be learned properly. What had to be done had to be done at once. Her brisk example helped to save a generation of pupils from the drag of procrastination.

I was not one of the brighter sparks. I was the new boy, late come to the class and not quite in step with the syllabus. I do not remember feeling out of place or overshadowed by those who did better, nor do I remember mornings when I had a sinking feeling about going to school as I had sometimes at schools in new buildings and with nicer teachers. The days passed briskly, Saturday came round quick. The class at the top of the school was bright with a certain pride in spite of the sombre hymns and the literature. We left to go on to our junior school without regret and without a parting word from the teacher. Nobody left an apple on her desk.

12 · ON SUNDAYS

I had Saturdays off. On Sunday I returned to the same high room which was used then by the junior department of Fulledge Wesleyan Methodist Sunday school. The teacher's desk had been shifted to what in weekdays was the side of the room, the piano was turned to a different angle, and at one end was erected a trestle table covered army fashion with a blanket. There our attendance was recorded in a register and acknowledged with a purple blob on a star card which was returned to us at the end of the proceedings as a kind of receipt. The star card marker wore tweed plus-fours which I took to be the garb of the trade like a boilerman's overalls or a coal miner's helmet. We sang hymns we could understand.

> The purple-headed mountain
> The river running by.
> The sunset and the morning
> That brighten up the sky.

Bright and beautiful. Streets ahead of the 'Though the darkness hide Thee' type of worship. The room was a different place from weekdays, full of warmth and kindness.

> I think when I read that sweet story of old,
> Of when Jesus was here amongst men,
> How he called little children as lambs to his fold,
> I should like to have been with Him then.

We sang usually without attention but sometimes the words gave a glimpse of an undiscovered country and filled us with a sweet sense of loss for what we had never known.

The instruction struck no such chords. It was imparted by a young lady who on weekdays was an assistant at a toy shop in Burnley town centre. She was accustomed to giving information from complicated catalogues about Meccano parts and Hornby accessories, and tackled the lesson in the teacher's handbook in the same factual and comprehensive way. She read out the whole lot, the text which was intended to be read out, suggestions intended for her guidance about what explanations to give and what questions to ask, and plugs for religious publications. She careered over plain type, black type, italics and parentheses like a heavy tank rolling hatch down over a variety of terrain and obstacles.

'A certain man went down from Jerusalem to Jericho and fell amongst thieves which stripped him of his raiment and wounded him and departed, leaving him half dead. Explain to the children the hardship of a journey before trams and buses and without proper roads. Do they know of rough paths? Can they describe a long walk? See the Holy Land 5 – A Rocky Path, set of twelve, Methodist Publications, 4½d. post free. And by chance there came down a certain priest that way . . .'

It was like watching a goat I had seen which had got at somebody's picnic carrier bag and downed the lot, sandwiches, wrapping paper, a bathing costume and finally the carrier itself. Our instructor, in fairness, did not profess to be a teacher. She was the accompanist and played the piano quite well, pedalling hard and acknowledging false notes with ladylike curses. She took the bottom class of the junior school as it were ex officio. Her deficiences were known. In the course of his rounds Mr Parrans the Sunday school secretary would come and crouch down in his pinstripes and with some humour sort out the story line from the instructions and commercials.

The Good Samaritan was a difficult one for him. It was not conceivable to us that a stricken person could be left in the road and certainly not that anybody would want to make off with his 'raiment'. Anyone we had seen keel over in the street was so populously succoured that he was more likely to succumb to manhandling than to neglect. And it would be years before we heard of places where people would pass by in case they were mugged themselves and of other places where they would take no notice in case the victim had been struck by the car of an apparatchik or dumped by the secret police. But we did know the Holy Land was a rough spot inhabited by foreigners and it was obvious that the first to pass by on the other side was a bad hat because he was a priest. Priests, by which we understood Roman Catholics, stood further beyond the pale than Tories, Anglicans and the supporters of Blackburn Rovers. The Levite, next on the scene, we knew nothing about but the name was clearly villainous. It was a shock then to learn from Mr Parrans that in Jesus' time these two characters were thought of as goodies and the Samaritan as a baddie, much as we might regard a German. I had a vision of the Good Samaritan in 'raiment' but surmounted by the German helmet which my father had retrieved from the battlefield and which now served as a receptable for auntie Abbie's boot-cleaning tackle.

There was great merriment about the two pence the Samaritan left for a week's board. In our time it was only enough to buy the Adventure, a two-ounce bar of chocolate or five Woodbines, but Mr Parrans held forth about the astonishing jaunts it would have financed in his youth 'when the Queen was on the throne', and offered a guess that in Jesus' time it would have kept a family of Hebrews for six weeks provided they did not smoke or drink. Rising, he apologised to our teacher for interrupting her. She said not at all, he had made things very clear. Then, eyes down, she rolled on into the lesson's conclusion, over the line of stars and the black rule and into the preview of next week's catalogue.

That was Sunday afternoon. On Sunday mornings we were given a scrappier sort of performance in Sunday school then marched across the cobbled yard to the chapel. It had been built in 1860 when Britannia ruled the waves and British cotton clothed the world. It was a mausoleum from which the spirit of those it commemorated had departed leaving a great emptiness: large opaque windows, dim chandeliers, 'no light,' as the poet said, 'but rather darkness visible', polished pews, and a high mahogany pulpit that placed the minister almost on the level of the encircling gallery.

They had us on parade ages before anything began. Sometimes we were even there before my grandfather, a notoriously early arriver, who passed the time feeling the water pipes, testing the window chords and welcoming the few arrivals at the door. It was none of his business, he held no office. We played such games as guessing the dates on each other's pennies brought for the collection. When we became noisy my grandfather looked across with raised eyebrows. It was a trick, I suppose, he had learned and abandoned in his unsuccessful attempt to subdue his daughters. Fulledge chapel brought out the worst in people.

It was, however, the circuit chapel, so we were largely spared the ministrations of local preachers, bigots who trudged down from Worsthorne and Dunnockshaw and in lesser chapels gave the small congregation of old ladies their Sunday roasting. It was usually the ordained minister who scaled the pulpit at Fulledge, the Reverend J.E. Howard, a kindly soul distinguished by steel-rimmed glasses like American business men wore. He gave the children a kind of mini sermon which started with some anecdote alleged to have occurred during the past week and containing humorous twists which left us cold but evoked a thin laugh from the adults sitting in isolated pairs in the expanse of the chapel. He reached the end of the story like a man reaching the top of a hill. 'Now,' he proclaimed, 'that rather reminds me of Jesus Christ'. Over the summit and down the other side, accelerating into an analogy which either because it was so tenuous or because of the speed of delivery we were unable to follow, and finally down to earth with some spectacle-flashing conclusion which so excited and delighted him that everybody in the chapel beamed.

We were allowed to leave before Mr Howard delivered his main oration but not before the freshness of the morning had passed while we sang a psalm which I inaccurately but rightly thought was called the Tedium. 'We praise Thee, O God, we acknowledge Thee to be the Lord. All the earth doth worship Thee, the Father everlasting.' And sure enough out of this dirge emerged the spectres that should have been boxed up in day school on Friday afternoon along with the reading books – cherubim and seraphim taking off for a weekend flight. It was not until several years later when we obtained a dictionary through a newspaper sales promotion campaign that I discovered who they were supposed to be. The cherubim, it transpired, were a reserve team, 'the second order of ninefold celestial hierarchy'. Seraphim were the first order but still a poor lot. In the weekday hymn the whole gang of them were described as 'falling down before Thee'. Their part in the Tedium was a long wail: 'To Thee cherubim and seraphim continually do cry'.

At the end of the psalm the congregation sank down. They collected our cash and let us go. My father waited outside with Eric. We went a walk and home for our Sunday dinner. It was a return to a warm and mellow world. Everybody was at home on Sundays. The doorsteps and window ledges had been freshly rubbing-stoned and smoke billowed from the rows of house chimneys. People moved at leisure in their best clothes. Even the men who exercised greyhounds on Towneley Holmes wore new caps. The recreation ground was empty. The industrial pall had settled over the town in gritty particles and when the sun shone the air was blue from roasting joints. It was familiar and welcoming and solid.

The chapel was spoken of as 'God's house'. The Sunday school at the opposite end of the yard I thought of as Jesus' house, not a complementary but a rival establishment. I was on Jesus' side though I knew he could be disagreeable at times. He was peevish, for instance, with the disciples, first recruiting them with such impatience that they were not allowed to say goodbye to their parents or go to a funeral, then, knowing them to be simple men, asking impossible conundrums and getting ratty when they did not know the answer. But they in turn did some daft things like fishing on the wrong side of the boat and telling the little children to clear off. Perhaps anybody would have got mad with them sometimes. Jesus was only human. He deserved a better dad.

God put the wind up you if you allowed yourself to think

about him. He had you taped. He could see you under the table, he knew if we skimped the polishing of carpet clips in the darkness of the stairs and he dished out punishment with a heavy hand. You could never be sure of going to heaven. It was not automatic like going on from Fulledge to Todmorden road day school. That did not worry me; I would gladly leave the place to the cherubim and seraphim. But he could incommode you here and now with any number of supernatural strokes. He could turn you into a pillar of salt, flood you out, have you laid on an altar or left in a pit, afflict you with boils, smash your tablets, bring buildings crashing down about your ears, strike you as bald as an egg and generally fix you up with such a bad time that you would be reduced to wailing and gnashing your teeth. The thunder was his voice. There was a picture in the family bible of Adam and Eve driven from the Garden of Eden under storm clouds which formed the features of an angry park keeper. We took good care in thunderstorms to open all doors so that any bolts aimed at us would bounce straight through the house and smash the windows in Admiral street. If you belonged to Pharaoh's host he would drown you. If you were of the other lot he would leave you tramping about in the desert for forty years incompetently misled and constantly upbraided by the worst kind of local preacher. He was boastful, jealous and vindictive, and he and his toadies moralised like school teachers.

My mother was able to make little inroad on this heresy. By 1931 Methodists had virtually abandoned theology for politics, so that in trying to dissuade me from seeing God and Jesus as opposing goal-keepers at opposite ends of the school yard my mother had little more grasp of the countervailing doctrine of the Trinity than the school children who sang about it each morning. She turned up a verse in the bible which seemed apposite to the general relationship. 'God so loved the world that he gave his only beloved son that whosoever believeth in him should not perish but have eternal life'. That seemed clear enough, but it was not Nonconformist practice to permit a poetic image to suffice. Explanation led to the proposition that Jesus died for our sins and in order to placate God. That made me think even more badly about God. My mother mentioned some of his good points; he created the heavens and earth without which none of us would be here and there would be no such places as Turf Moor football ground, the Pentridge pictures and Blackpool. Jesus got on very well with God really, the crucifixion apart. He referred to his home as 'my father's house'. He did not have separate premises but lived there on full board. He looked after the place when God was away. I had a vision of an attendant alone in a public baths on closing day. I thought Jesus deserved better.

These ponderings were of no weight. The passing of the year was agreeably marked by religious feast days, and Sunday school workers excelled at making them enjoyable for us: Easter, when the spring sun paled the chapel chandeliers; the Harvest Festival when the chapel was filled with a thanks offering of greengrocery and my grandfather took vegetable marrows on which our names pricked small on the young plant had stretched like the lettering on an airship; Christmas when we had the bunscuffle and the tree. There were feasts of more recent origin: the Sunday school anniversary when migrants returned and the moribund were brought to chapel and those who were going to get them got new clothes; the field day when we trooped behind a brass band and the banner to Towneley park; the days given over to home and foreign missions.

The home mission was a rather thin occasion. The town missioner, Mr James Quirk, who looked like an undertaker and toiled for the uplift of the poor, received our gifts of broken toys and incomplete jigsaws and rewarded us with a sanctimonious account of the squalor in which his clients wallowed. The celebration of the foreign mission was much more exciting. We assembled buzzing like a football crowd in the big room. On to the stage came Mr Parrans, the Reverend Mr Howard, men in pin stripes and ladies in tweeds and in the middle of them, like a boxer approaching among his handlers, a different-looking man, the returned Christian soldier brown from the sun or yellow from quinnine. He launched into a situation report. We knew whom he was talking about. We had no idea who were 'the poor' in Burnley to whom Mr Quirk ministered. The missionary's customers we knew well, 'natives' who were prominently represented in groups shown in prints lending a willing ear to Jesus and present as subject races in books once given as Sunday school prizes. Times were changing. The empire was failing, the will had perished, enlightenment prevailed. Nobody spoke of knocking anybody into shape. We still sang:

> I'll be a shepherd to those lambs
> And cast their idols all away.

But it was reluctantly acknowledged that the lambs might not want their idols cast away. It was a hymn of an earlier time and in fairness the determination to do things for people's benefit whether they liked it or not was a general Wesleyan precept not specifically directed at 'natives'. We would equally have closed the pubs for the benefit of drinkers and arrested bookies' runners for the benefit of gamblers. The less they liked it the more good it would do them.

This dominating aspect of righteousness was now played down by missionaries. They were different from the gaunt men who had left their bones in the bush, young, clean-shaven and humorous, no longer the consuls of God and the

Queen but rather publicity officers and fund raisers for their flocks. The accounts they brought back from diverse parts of the dark continent were agreeably similar in content like some films of the time all shot on the same sets and with much the same characters. There was the mission and the village and one location outside. Just as cowboy films had the same rocks to be shot off, so all missionary accounts had a log across a crocodile-infested river to teeter on. Journeys began and ended above the snapping jaws. The cast always included an uncle Tom to whom our hearts warmed and a proud pagan warrior chief who, after some unpleasantness in which he nearly got our missionary into the pot, was brought to an acknowledgment of God's supremacy and benevolence through some such circumstance as the restoration to health of his little daughter for whom witch doctors brought from near and far had cast spells in vain.

Once in the fold, the natives proved to have spiritual qualities lacking in us. Their telepathic powers, which might once have been exercised in pursuit of sorcery, were now put to sensible use, so that a servant who had been left with no idea of what day or week Bwana would return from the bush would have the bed made, the bible dusted and the kettle on the primus stove at the very moment when our lecturer and his train of porters were crossing the log over the crocodile-infested river on the last lap of their journey. Others of the flock were reported as developing on more conventional lines. One had learned to play the organ by ear in remarkably short time, another to diagnose simple maladies and to dole out aspirins and laxatives with restraint and in less than the explosive quantities demanded by the patients. The schools prospered and in some every boy in the class was bent on being ordained as a minister. The missionary paused. Mr Parrans and the Reverend J.E. Howard up on the platform started a laugh and all of us in the body of the hall joined in. At the time we all thought it was meant as a joke.

Leaving Africa behind in Sunday school and returning to our sombre streets was as saddening as leaving the western prairies behind in the Pentridge pictures. My heart turned to becoming a missionary. I volunteered to be a collector for the foreign field, and was given a sealed wooden box with pictures of natives on the outside. At the year end the boxes were returned and opened and an investiture held at which gold stars were pinned by the missionary on the lapels of those who had collected five pounds and medals of baser metal for smaller amounts. There was a cut-off point, I think at three pounds, and below that all you got was his best thanks.

When I arrived home with the box my parents did not know quite what to say. The next day my mother explained that it would not be sufficient to leave it where I had set it on the mantlepiece in mute appeal to visitors; collectors were expected to persuade a number of relatives and family friends to subscribe weekly. I could see no reason why that should not be done. She explained that our family and friends, though fervent for foreign missions, were too impecunious to support them more tangibly than by prayer. Winning medals was a hobby for the well-off. Were we not well off? No. It was the first time I had heard anything of the sort. Were we poor? Yes. Then why did we take broken toys for the poor to Mr Quirk? They were even poorer, they were destitute. I delved no deeper into the class structure. I took the box round to everybody we knew. They all gave me something; uncle Ben and Jack Yates even dropped in silver threepennies. But it was clear that for everybody it was a once and for all donation. There were already too many club collectors announcing themselves down the hall on Friday nights. The box was put out of sight on the gas meter in our parlour which was unfurnished and used only for indoor football and games with a balloon. On the Sunday I had to return it my father rather crossly fed in coins like an addict at a one-armed bandit until my mother restrained him. We had no idea how much had accumulated. The missionary presented medals to those who had brought £3 and over, then Mr Parrans read the names and amounts of lesser collectors in descending order of merit. I was last. 'Donald Haworth,' he said, looking over his spectacles and with the slow finality of the last announcement, 'two and eleven pence'.

There was a silence. Mr Parrans smirked, struggled to

control himself, snorted through clenched teeth along the fuse of a laugh and exploded. The Reverend Mr Howard laughed. The missionary laughed. Everybody on the platform laughed and everybody in the hall. Boys slapped me on the back, girls batted their eyes, as though it were not a failure but a roguish kind of success. I remember the event with pleasure. All the same it put paid to my ambition to be a missionary.

Once a year the children gave in chapel a kind of concert aimed at advertising the virtues. We sang and declaimed from the stage set up in front of the pulpit. Sometimes we subjected the congregation to a random ragbag of warnings and exhortations, more often the precepts were related to a theme which developed along with a construction project. We built a large model from blocks labelled courage, honesty, faith and so forth, stopping after placing each block to speak a homily or sing a relevant hymn. A favoured model was a lighthouse, in which at the finale the lantern lit up and a boy with a resonant voice would proclaim: 'Jesus said, I am the light of the world. Let your light so shine before men that they may see your good works, and glorify your Father which is in heaven.' Old ladies sighed with indulgent admiration and younger mothers with relief that nobody had been electrocuted. The congregation rose to sing the final hymn which invariably was Bunyan's 'To be a pilgrim'.

For this and for this alone we had been coached by the chapel organist Mr Hedges who came down specially from the eyrie in the gallery he shared with the pigeons. He was remote from everybody up there with his back to the chapel and screened by a curtain, round which he peered to scowl at the Reverend Howard's back if the sermon went on too long. He had a bald head, steel-rimmed glasses and a burnt walrus moustache, a man of an earlier time, something like Kipling in appearance. He disdained to accompany the lighthouse part of the business. For that our teacher and her piano had to be hoisted to the platform where she performed nervously and with muttered vexation at her errors. Mr Hedges would have no truck. He was distant, aloof and rather frightening.

Moreover he was at odds with my grandfather. He played the hymns at one tempo, my grandfather sang them at another. When the music permitted him to free one hand from the keyboard he twisted up over his curtain and glared down into the body of the chapel. My grandfather ignored him and deliberately turned as he sang to direct his fire into all quarters. Mr Hedges switched in the supercharger. My grandfather raised his voice. It was an unseemly uproar, enough to bring thumping wakefulness to backsliders sleeping it off half a mile away. The Reverend Mr Howard, exposed up in his vibrating pulpit, tried with a sawing hand to strike a compromise tempo. Others in the sparse congregation either gave up or came close to a nervous breakdown. On one of the special occasions when the chapel was full and the service ended with the singing of a rousing evangelical hymn my grandfather was inspired to start the chorus off again. Hundreds of voices joined him while the upstaged organ remained silent and Mr Hedges' bald head popped up and down over his curtain like a ping-pong ball in a shooting booth. He let them finish unaccompanied then when they were just about to subside to their seats he struck up the chorus again. They rose again and sang, the old and feeble visibly wilting. It could have gone on all night, but the moment the second repeated chorus finished Mr Howard brought down the axe on proceedings with the blessing. 'May the grace of our Lord Jesus Christ,' he bellowed, 'the love of God and the fellowship of the Holy Spirit be with you and remain with you always'. Visitors always said they had enjoyed a good sing.

We were rather apprehensive when Mr Hedges came across to the Sunday school to tutor us for the Bunyan hymn. He turned out to be a scholar of charm wholly immersed in his subject. He read the lines of 'To be a pilgrim' and encouraged us to interpret the meaning. He asked us to hear the tramp of heavy vowels through the line 'Hobgoblin nor foul fiend shall daunt his spirit' and the dawning light in the next line 'He knows he at the end shall life inherit'. He sang the lines with different stresses and at different tempos. He presented the Christian life as a journey, an adventure and a crusade. Hobgoblins and foul fiends were not to be disbelieved in. Nor were they to be feared. They were to be sought out and smitten at all times and wherever they might be found. We sang the hymn well at the first attempt. We sang it better on the day. From the elevation of the stage I could see the dome of his head above the curtain. At the end both hands shot up alongside in triumph. We did not have the pleasure of his tuition for another year.

13 · UNDER THE DOCTOR

Leaving Fulledge day school was like coming out of prison.
Todmorden road junior school was a low building with
wide windows and so new that the stones had not yet
blackened. Our new teacher was young and polished and
elegant. She came down hard on the poor. She assailed them
for black finger nails and wiping their nose on their sleeve,
and at the first sign of head-scratching she summoned a
woman bureaucrat addressed as nurse who inspected the
whole class and gave us notes to take home requiring the
nits to be combed out. The teacher particularly abhorred a
frail cross-eyed girl in rags called Hilda, for whom the
headmaster had obtained a big carton of cod liver oil and
malt. It was kept in the teacher's cupboard. At playtimes
Hilda stood on a chair and spooned herself a dose out. It
was not easily managed. The shelves became sticky, then
some of the desk tops and books. It was like living on fly
paper. The teacher ranted at the child. The class sat silent.
Annoyance or anger we would have understood, but there
was a note of repulsion which shocked us. Hilda did not
react; she never did. But I felt ashamed to be one of the
teacher's monitors. After consulting my grandfather who
had the grace to take children seriously I returned my badge.
The teacher shopped me. Evidently she had seen the report
that raised the question of my hearing and now she caught
me breathing through my mouth. 'Look at him sitting with
his mouth wide open again,' she would shrill out. It was
retaliation rather than diagnosis but when the schools' doctor
came he looked from a report in her handwriting to my

open mouth and gave my mother a sealed note which was passed without our seeing it round a conspiracy of quacks and landed me on the operating table at Victoria hospital to have my tonsils and adenoids removed.

I knew it would be rather nasty because my mother was at pains to make light of it. She had had the same operation in Liverpool as a child and her prevailing memory was of having been kept awake by a younger child who repeatedly asked to be allowed home. That was something I would not have to put up with because I was not to be kept overnight. It was further hinted that admission to hospital was to be regarded not as a sentence but as a privilege, and indeed I knew that my father had put on his best suit to see Jack Yates who used his influence in the Labour movement to get me admitted. We arrived as required before dawn and waited for hours before I was taken to an ante-room and undressed. Boredom had stilled my own fear. My mother crouched before me holding together the ends of the blanket she had draped over my shoulders and trembled with anxiety. It seemed overdone. I did not yet know how much less governable than our own fear is the apprehension we feel for others.

I came round, nose and mouth full and oozing into a tin that had been placed against my cheek. I was taken home in a taxi and lay in my parents' big bed feeling very ill until I threw up the chloroform. The room reeked as though there was a gas leak. My father, home from work, came up and said he heard I had given the surgeon a roasting. Apparently a kind orderly or cleaner, seeing my mother anxious in the waiting room, told her I had gone under cursing the anaesthetist and quoted a sample of the dialogue. My mother was shocked but accepted the report in the spirit it was offered as evidence of a fighting temperament that would not easily expire upon the table.

Uncle Ben arrived in the evening with a wooden fort he had made. It had been intended for Stanley who had readily agreed that I should have it instead. He would; he had at seven a mature generosity which some people never achieve in a lifetime. I sensed the asymmetry of injustice; my

indisposition would be temporary but he would be permanently deprived of the fort. I croaked something of the sort.
Uncle Ben said not at all, Donny. He'd knock another up in
double quick time. I knew he wouldn't. Adults rarely kept
promises. A repeat performance was unheard of.

I was awakened next morning by the burble of voices in
the hall passage below. Visitors spoke in muted inquiry. My
mother responded. Restive night but sleeping now. Couldn't
take anything for breakfast. Try him soon with half an egg
beaten up in warm milk. The voices sounded strange and it
was not only because I was drowsy and my head thick. The
speech was like something heard in a dream or in a sanctified
place, muted, solemn and reverential, call and response in
the ritual obeisance that was made to illness. My mother
went in dread of illness. When it came it gave her status and
a part to play prescribed by custom.

The health of the whole nation was poor. Many of the best
had been lost in youth, to emigration which ran at the rate
of nearly 300,000 a year before 1914, and to the war which
claimed more than 700,000 young lives. The population of
1931 included some four million who had been unfit for
military service and 1.5 million who had come back permanently weakened by wounds or gas. In winter coughing
filled public places, cinemas, chapels, the football stand, the
reading room in the library. In Dr Dixon's waiting room
benches of men sat in the light of a low fire coughing like a
hacking caricature of a band. The daytime streets were full
of men on crutches. Every other house seemed to have an
old woman invalid permanently installed in the parlour.

Mothers of young children lived in fear of illness. When
they themselves were small death had claimed 150 children
in every thousand at birth. By 1930 infant mortality had
been reduced to 67 per thousand live births. Sanitation had
improved, but nutrition was poor, worse in our area than it
had been in the prosperous days of a generation ago. It was
reckoned that a fifth of all children in Britain were chron-
ically ill-nourished and half the population suffered from
diet deficiency. Neither I nor my brother ever went hungry
and we grew up strong, but our mother went through bad

years when she had colds and influenza every winter. One
day she collapsed in a public wash house where she had
started to take the clothes and was brought home by ambulance. I overheard a woman warning her it would do no
good to give up food to us if it deprived us of a mother.

Epidemic diseases still carried off thousands of children
every winter. The fever hospital had its own distinctive
ambulance which we were instructed not to go near. When
it came for Peter O'Donovan we were allowed to stand
across the street outside cousin Stanley's house and shout
good luck when he was carried out on the shoulder of the
ambulance man. He pulled down the blanket which encircled
the lower part of his face and croaked a line from a song,
'Does Santa Claus sleep with his whiskers under or over the
sheet?' The ambulance rocked away down the unpaved
street. Men from the sanitary inspectors' department came
and fumigated the house. People who had not been there
were told of Peter's quotation as evidence of his spirit. He
died three weeks later. The serum that attacked diptheria
also attacked the heart. Many children were cured of the
disease but killed.

It is perhaps not surprising that concern about illness grew
morbid. Threats to health were seen everywhere. The berries
in the hedge and the fungus plants in the fields were poison.
Cuts 'turned septic'. If you sucked a pencil you could die of
lead poisoning. Pips and seeds accidentally swallowed could
start a growth. Chewing gum could inflate you like an
inner tube. On the other hand when my father accidentally
swallowed some of the nails he kept in his mouth at work it
was deflation through puncturing that had to be feared or, if
not that, the danger of rusting from the inside. A snuffle or
a stomach ache was searchingly questioned. Throats were
peered into. Children often at first denied and then admitted
in a flood of tears symptoms they thought would kill them.
A generation grew up so afflicted by hypochrondria that in
its time it supplanted the Royal Navy as the prime object of
the nation's esteem with the National Health Service.

When my mother was a child there was still the fear that
troubled Shakespeare's Romans of the 'vile contagion of the
night . . . the rheumy and unpurged air'. In winter, as I

have mentioned, my grandfather used to place a blanket on a clothes maiden round the children's bed to deflect the vapours. That theory was now scorned by the enlightened and replaced by an opposite and more uncomfortable faith in the wind. New schools were designed with enough window space for the tropics. In the interests of sound health everybody was frozen stiff. At places where they had to compete for custom they had more sense. One of the small incidental pleasures of Saturday pictures after a week of exposure at school was the warm scented fug which tumbled visibly in the projector beam. I knew some children who were made to breathe at an open bedroom window, sucking in air through a glass tube to purify it, and a young man who breathed in the morning air as he performed with dumbbells, but he had applied to enter the ministry and it was only one of several eccentricities he adopted including wearing a bowler hat. At most homes the draughts were thought sufficient to ventilate the place. Some of our window cords were brittle with disuse. Once in struggling to open a bedroom window we dislodged a shower of hardened soot from the top of the sash and saw the gas mantle on the wall bracket flutter to pieces in the breeze. That put an end to fresh air. In winter it was not air we lacked but heat. There was only one fire in the house burning in a small grate made even smaller by firebricks placed at each side to save coal. On cold evenings we sat round with our feet in the hearth and the cat eventually settled on the cinders.

When we were caught in the rain on the way to school we remained wet for most of the morning or afternoon because of the absorbency of our heavy clothing and the open windows. The cloakroom stank of wet coats. At home we changed in front of the fire into old clothes brought down warm from the cistern cupboard. Children whose mother worked went back to a cold house and remained clammy. The crucial area to keep dry, we learned, was the feet because the blood went straight from them to the heart, which would run rough like a cold engine. In fact few children suffered from wet feet because some had welling-tons and the clogs worn by the rest were less vulnerable to deterioration than shoes. It seemed to rain or snow all winter because of our damp clothing and also because the sun was permanently cut out by an overcast of smoke. That was a health hazard which nobody thought about at the time and which was not tackled for another thirty years.

Purging was the main defence against illness, a thorough scumpering out, as my grandfather termed the treatment. My brother and I were actually dosed once with the notorious Victorian nostrum, brimstone and treacle, a sodden gravel of dirty grey. We were given liquid paraffin which is like drinking oil, and Senna pods and Epsom salts which being astringent at least do not make one heave. As a special treat we were dosed with cascara sagrada, a superior kind of laxative which a lady who was a friend of my grandmother's friend Mrs Corbett and a matron in a hospital recommended and used. When we resisted, these charges were smuggled into our food and drink, reducing us to such suspicion that we circled uncontaminated dishes like dogs that have burned their nose ends.

My father who was never ill found illness and the cult of sickness distasteful. He also hated fuss. He would try to take no notice of the plaintive negotiations we conducted with our mother about the measure of the medicine to be taken and the kind of sweet or the size of the jam spoon to follow, then suddenly he would fling his Shoe and Leather News across the room and ferociously round on us. 'Get it down, lad, or I'll pour it down.' The next moment he would have us by the nose end, pouring part of the nostrum into our gaping mouth and the rest over our shoulders and boots.

The nastiest brew I had poured down me was Balm of Gilead which bubbled away in my stomach through an evening in the pictures, renewing its poisonous taste in belches. It was a cough cure; it gave me stomach ache. My mother concluded not that balm itself was wrong but that forcing it down prevented it from doing a good office. She would not condemn it; it was a herb, some sort of biblical sanction hung about its name. My grandmother had a religious belief that there was a herb in the field to cure every malady which benefice was evidenced by the invariable growth of healing docks close to stinging nettles. If you

pointed to the columns of the week's departed in the paper
or to Jack Yates at his wits' end in February to get enough
coffins knocked up to maintain the Co-op's funeral service,
she would repeat that the herbs existed but remained to be
discovered. Many people partook of herbs. There were
enough in our district alone to keep a herbalist's shop
in business. My grandmother got nice herbs, elder and
peppermint from which a scented hot drink was brewed and
cayenne pods which dropped in tea pleasantly scorched your
throat and made my grandfather purr and roar gently in bed
in the morning.

The declared enemy was germs. People breathed them at
you, dogs carried them, they came enveloped in bad smells.
At home as a pre-emptive strike we poured a disinfectant
that smelled like creosote down the drains to put paid to
them where they cowered, and during epidemics we gargled
with some stuff called Condy's Fluid, silver crystals of
potassium permanganate which dissolved to make water
look like raspberry pop. A handful was chucked into our
bath to grapple with exterior germs. In sick rooms an onion
was hung up to absorb the germs, which it clearly had done
when it went black. When the sickness had passed the room
or the whole house was fumigated by burning sulphur on a
shovel which wracked the inmates and asphixiated the last
remaining germs.

I was slow in getting the hang of germs. I thought they
had something to do with Germans who were also not well
thought of at the time. My mother showed me a picture of
a germ on the disinfectant label, an impish insect kind of
chap to whom I rather warmed. It was not to be taken
literally, she said, it was only an illustration. Real germs did
not have rolling black eyes. They were minute, invisible
and multitudinous. On dirty hands there could be hundreds
which would ride on your jam butty down to your vital
organs. They lived in dirt but were not of the dirt. She saw
we were headed towards the kind of theological shallows on
which we had foundered before. She changed course. A
man, she said, had drowned in the canal and the doctor told
the coroner he had swallowed hundreds of germs. Would
that matter, I asked, if he had already been drowned? She

conceded that it seemed like a case of overkill; he had been doubly dealt with. But it was characteristic of germs to operate as a second wave of attack; they often came and gave the coup de grâce to unwary people at the very moment when they believed themselves to be on the road to recovery.

The gritty cuts to our knees and elbows which we frequently suffered on the cinders of the recreation ground were treated with Sanitas and later with iodine, a pungent and more manly disinfectant which made us howl. My father was good at applying it. He would do it swiftly and grip the limb and sometimes our shoulders with a firmness that eased the sting. One afternoon when I came home from school he was sitting by the fire, which was a shock because it was not time to be home from work. He was pale and the room smelled of iodine. A hand had been mangled at work in the stitching machine. He had walked a mile to the doctor's surgery, where Harry Dixon poured iodine over his hand and bandaged it so heavily that he was unable to go back and resume work. He had beautiful hands which had soothed me in pain and which I had often watched as he worked. I was moved by pity for his hand, but I tried to match his calm and asked if it had hurt when the iodine was poured on. He said it did a bit at the time. He said no more about it. It was in great contrast to the drama generally made of illness and injury. One or two visitors left looking as though they had been short-changed.

We often had 'gatherings', painful subcutaneous infections which are now dispelled by antibiotics but which then had to be drawn to a head by bathing and poultices. It was a long process which at each treatment left the inflamed area hot and throbbing. Lint was applied sodden with boiling water, and poultices of linseed, kaolin and sometimes cum-frey, a 'herb' which was boiled like a cabbage, squeezed out in a bandage and clapped on the spot. All poultices oozed. Burns were treated with cold poultices of tea leaves. Coughs were cured or prevented by rubbing the chest with camphor-ated oil or wintergreen, earaches with warm olive oil and all strains with Sloan's linament which had a re-assuring picture on the label of a man with a handlebar moustache. We were encouraged to breathe in the fumes of coal tar from the

boilers used in repairing the roads and to eat plenty of
beetroot which 'made blood'. We wore a sachet of camphor
on a string round our neck and were dosed after meals with
cod liver oil and malt. Refinements developed. The camphor
bag was replaced by an 'iodine locket', a tiny tin case which
was claimed to house a powerful general prophylactic. The
cod liver oil and malt was superceded by proprietory sugar-
coated pills, said to contain a 'concentrate'. They cost money
that should have gone on food. Nobody was to know.
Advertisements could say anything. No public advice was
ever given against a commercial product. Doctors declined
to be drawn into opinions. They would have been on
marshy ground; their own medicine was scarcely more
effective and just as expensive.

A couple of brushes with doctors passed into the family
lore. My grandmother's father William Rylance, a colliery
shot-firer, went to the doctor in Whiston about 1880 to seek
a cure for his persistent indigestion. The doctor stood him
against a wall, asked him to open his waistcoat, stepped
back across the room and charged, punching the patient in
the stomach with such force that his knees buckled and the
long-imprisoned wind escaped in a roar. It was felt that the
treatment, although effective, offended against the aesthetics
of the healing art.

In our own time grandfather Sephton was given a pum-
melling when he went to have his rheumatism treated at a
hospital at Buxton where the Weavers' Union had a number
of places which they generously shared with non-members.
He took with him as required new flannel pyjamas and a
pair of real football shorts which he promised on parting
should be mine some day along with his watch. He was
distressed to find that the shorts were all he was permitted
to wear during parts of the therapy. He was even obliged to
discard his chest protector, a padded sort of jerkin worn
next to the skin which never came off between October and
May. Their manners distressed him. He had never before
been in a hospital nor even in the army or prison. The
brusque commands, the conversation about his case which

ignored his presence and repelled any attempted contribution, the use of his surname without the honorific to
which he had been accustomed from youth created indignation which was fuelled by the belief that these discourtesies
flourished because the patients were there by charity. He
was exhibited in his football shorts to a gang of medical
students, revolved before them, lectured over and prodded.
A superior medicine man stepped forward and dealt him
several sharp blows. Another excruciated him with the balls
of his thumbs. My grandfather rose. 'I came here to be
cured not to be hurt,' he announced and stalked out of the
shocked lecture room. He bought some picture postcards
and sticks of rock to bring home, passed a couple of waiting
hours in a park with some tramps whose acquaintance he
had made and caught the afternoon train out.

Doctors who actually assaulted patients were regarded as
exceptional but all doctors were feared. People were craven
in their presence. For the doctor's visit women polished the
house as though it was a museum and put on their best
clothes and accents. They apologised for troubling him.
They babbled all the way upstairs about the development of
the symptoms and the measures they had taken. They hoped
for a word of commendation and dreaded a rebuke. When
the doctor left, there was relief and jubilation as though the
holidays had begun. Books and toys came out. People
breezed in from neighbouring houses to hear what he had
said. Everybody brewed up.

Nobody I knew of ever challenged the doctor's bills.
Employed people were treated under national insurance,
panel patients, and got their medicine cheap. Everybody
else was a private patient. I do not know how doctors'
charges related to those of other professions but they were
high in relation to the resources of their patients. A bottle of
doctor's medicine seems to have cost nearly as much as a
week's food. In a survey of the time spending on food per
head is estimated at 3 shillings a week among the poor and 6
shillings among the 'most affluent'. An adult's bottle of
medicine cost 3s. 6d. and a child's 2s. 6d. Harry Dixon
dispensed two standard bottles, one containing bismuth for
stomach disorders and one containing chlorodine for coughs.

To his credit he also had a second bottle for coughs, a red syrup which looked and tasted nice. Medicine for panel patients was dispensed to prescription by the chemist. The rest the doctor mixed himself. He would tramp heavily along the corridor and through the dark waiting room to a partitioned corner where you could hear him grunting and wheezing above the clink of stoppers and the glug of liquid. He could have five panel patients back in the street clutching their prescriptions in the time it took him to deal with one private patient. There was a convention that we should go in the daytime and leave the evenings to the workers. The surgery was like a club or a pub to them. Some old men went in to keep warm and enjoy the company. Harry Dixon who was known as a good sport did not mind, but his caretaker, a crone even he feared, would burst in whenever laughter rose or anyone dared to poke the fire, and turn out all who were not the night's genuine customers. Above the street door glowed a dull purple lamp, a trademark Harry Dixon's father had installed when electricity first arrived.

Panel patients had to watch their step. The doctor had the power to send them back to work. Private patients had an opposite anxiety, to bring the treatment to an end before they were ruined. Illnesses were of long duration. Few specific remedies were known and natural recuperation was as often delayed as assisted by the treatment. Whatever was wrong the patient was put to bed and his rations cut off. Bed seemed right because it was the only warm place in winter, but having got you there the doctor did not let you out in a hurry. Your rations were daintily restored through many stages, a little strained broth, a small piece of steamed hake, half an egg beaten up in milk, jellied chicken, salmon, a little chopped carrot, a carton of fresh cream. Patients thus enfeebled by malnutrition would see mirages of steaming potatoes and Yorkshire pudding, which might be taken for delirium and a reason for straining the broth even thinner. Then there was a long process of acclimatization, even for children with minor infections, that would begin with a half hour sitting by the fire with a blanket over the shoulders and work up to a short walk round the block if it wasn't too cold. The patient was left half-starved and shaky from lack of food and exercise and the family broke from the cost of the doctor and the special food.

Harry Dixon always then insisted on a period of convalescence. He would pull back the lower eyelid and detect slight anaemia, narrowing his own eyes with concern and against the smoke of his Turkish cigarette. Mothers tried to forestall him by speaking of the beetroot, cod liver oil and Ovaltine they were poised to buy. Undistracted, he would then thoughtfully examine the patient's other eyelid for confirmation and ask if somebody could come to the evening surgery to collect a tonic. It was yellow and contained iron in such quantities that if you didn't brush after every dose it plated your teeth. Four, five, six bottles of tonic were not unusual. It was the link Harry Dixon used to keep business turning over from one illness to the next.

My grandfather played the same part in family illness as he did in our house removals, a supervising and executive role which excluded tidying up bedrooms or reading aloud from picture books. He was an expert in illness, having been laid low by every known disease from his infancy, when his life was despaired of, to his sixty-third year. Retirement then proved the cure that had eluded him through his lifetime and, apart from rheumatism and bronchitis which afflicted everybody over sixty, he enjoyed health and mobility until his sudden death at 79. Not rude health. He looked after himself. He kept his boots sound and changed out of wet clothes. He wore a nightcap in bed and his quilted chest warmer over a layer of Thermogene all winter. On cold days he went to the football match with a hot water bottle buttoned to the waist of his trousers. He thought of delicate health as a sort of refinement. Grandad Haworth, he said, didn't have enough sense to be ill.

Premonition of illness in the family visited him through a dream in which battalions of insects crossed a window pane. He would arrive unsummoned on the door step, stay for a while with the invalid and saunter off to town in search of the cheaper delicacies, fish, a rabbit, marrow bones from which broth was made, and also to hire from the Co-op a set of crockery for the sick room. It included a bed pan, urine bottle and a feeding cup with a spout from which the moribund could be topped up. It was intended for the gravely ill but through the good offices of Jack Yates we were able to hire at such advantageous rates that the set arrived clinking in a carrier if anybody so much as went down with a bad cold. The time came when we simply did not return it. I had the impression we had won it outright like three-time winners of the Lonsdale Belt.

My grandfather came and went on errands throughout the first day of illness and as a finale to his exertions went to the doctor's surgery in the evening to fetch the medicine which would have been mixed and left on the mantlepiece of the waiting room. Quite against the practice and intention he would drop into the consulting room for a confidential word on the case with the doctor who must at first have been too astonished to take offence. They became pals. Harry Dixon greeted him alone of his patients across the street from the window of his car. He took to addressing him as 'grandpa'.

One day my grandfather arrived with a small electrical machine for the treatment of his rheumatism which had been surrendered to the Co-op as part payment of a funeral bill and appropriated by Jack Yates. We spent many happy and excruciating hours with it. It was worked by a big battery. The current, amplified by a coil, passed through two brass handles which the patient clutched and hence through his body. The coil was concealed inside a horizontal green cylinder and fitted with an adjustable core by which the current could be regulated. As it was withdrawn the hum of the machine rose to a high-pitched whine and the tingling in the hands developed into muscular convulsions which finally so knotted the fingers that it became impossible to let go of the handles. The current, we were led to believe, was little short at full bore of what was supplied to clients in Sing Sing. My brother and I timidly competed to reach quite low gradations, flinging away the handles the moment the tingling increased. My grandfather worked up steadily. People came in to watch him. He would increase the current little by little, waiting at each stage to permit his trembling body to absorb the extra charge, until at last the core was

wholly withdrawn and the machine screaming like a jet
engine. He bounced up and down in his seat with his quiff
swishing and his boots chattering on the floor. He then gave
his feet a do by immersing them in a bowl of brine into
which one of the handles of the machine was placed. He
tied a knob of flannel to a handle and rubbed it soaked in
brine round troublesome spots. He tried it on a piece of iron
which had got under the skin of a finger when he was a
blacksmith's striker and he attempted to restore animation
to the side of his face which had been stiffened by a stroke
when he was fifty. He rubbed our bruises with the damp
flannel knob; it was quite soothing. For himself he sought a
way to increase the current still further. A bigger battery
failed. So did some tinkering with the coil. He decided to
wait until he went back to auntie Abbie's where he could
wire himself into the mains. We had only gas, which was
fortunate for him because in the meantime he heard of a
man in Accrington who had followed the same notion and
cured his rheumatism and all other ills for ever.

My father was impatient with sickness. He could not bear
to listen to symptoms not only because he suspected
malingering but also because the ritual manner of reciting
them, detailed, sensitive and suffering, grated on his soul.
Once the doctor had authenticated our illness with a name
my father relented and treated us gently but when the tonic
stage was reached that for him was the end. He wanted to
hear no more about it. We were on parade at school the next
Monday morning. Grandfather Sephton, as I mentioned,
thought the Haworths lacking in refinement in this respect,
dating from an occasion when he had presented grandad
Haworth with a bottle of his own cough medicine. Half the
bottle, he said, would be enough to fettle him. Grandad
Haworth who had never been ill before welcomed such a
ready remedy. He drew the cork, swigged half the bottle
and handed it back with his thanks.

His was the more usual attitude among men. Illness was
not spoken of, symptoms were concealed or, if that was
impossible, passed off in a joke. George Formby's father
who suffered from tuberculosis set a style for those with

coughs. Rather than let it stop him he incorporated it into his act. He reeled about the stage fighting a comic battle with his cough. It became his partner, his straight man, in a double act. Men with bad chests used the technique modified to the occasion. It became second nature to add a comic flourish to any cough.

Most permanent invalids were women. They had a harder life than men, especially those who worked in the mills, and they were worn out earlier. It may also have been that bed was the only sanctioned refuge from unrelenting work. Some stayed there for years with illnesses that were never diagnosed. Once the prospect of long illness was established the bed was brought down to the living room or parlour where the patient could share the fire and be more easily attended by her daughter or daughter-in-law. The ordinary furniture, the armchairs and the sideboard with its wedding photographs, usually remained in the room pushed back against the wall. There was nowhere else to store them and perhaps they were left as a hopeful reminder that the arrangement was not intended to be permanent.

It worked well as long as the patient was, as they said, better side out. She would help with sedentary household jobs such as peeling potatoes and knit and mend clothes. She enjoyed the presence of the daughter, the coming and going of friends, doorstep salesmen and club collectors, and the company of grandchildren after school. When she declined what had kept up her spirits became wearying. Her presence could dwindle almost to that of an old dog sleeping in the corner. People spoke to her as though they were addressing a child. The doctor discussed her case over her head. Family conferences were held on the other side of the door. What she feared was to be shipped into the municipal hospital and to die among strangers. There was grave social disapproval of this course. I am sure the municipal hospital was a cheerier place than many houses but it was greatly feared by old people because it was indistinguishable in their minds from the adjoining workhouse. Most old people feared any hospital because of the dread that they might be operated on. Some especially feared the 'workhouse hospital' because of its reputation among the very old for dispatching patients in the night with a black bottle of poison.

Some invalids were not victims but tyrants. They subdued their families by force of character or by the threat of leaving their small savings to distant relations or the dogs' home, and often bamboozled them with precepts derived from Christian belief and tortuously and unanswerably argued. Most people had knocked off going to church by 1930 but few could bring themselves to challenge the authority on which these self-serving moralities were claimed to be based. They were out of their depth. They were outgunned, browbeaten and shamed. Some old ladies passed the long hours building up their fire power from tracts and the scriptures. They could also summon physical reinforcements in the form of combat groups from the churches, particularly the hot-gospel tabernacles, who went round visiting the indisposed faithful with hymns and prayers and held themselves ready on request to bring erring relatives to heel and repentance.

I can remember few old men among the permanent invalids in front rooms. Old men were turned out in the hours of daylight. The town was full of them. Air and exercise kept them fit and the social life of the streets kept up their spirits. Their illness was bronchitis which did not count. When it became chronic it killed them. They did not linger in the parlour. Ladies did not have the same tradition of dying with their boots on.

14 · CATHOLICS

Not all the families in our street were of industrial workers. There were two men who went to work in trilbies and came home clean. Mr Riley was an eccentric who lived alone. He always looked as though the wind had hit him. His hat was clapped on the back of a head of wild white hair, his tie a flapping lanyard, his trousers hoist six inches above his shoes. He moved in short gallops as though propelled by faulty electric batteries. He was said to be a clock maker, nobody knew where, and he was bad at regulating his own time. He never went anywhere without having to spurt. He knocked over children on tricycles, scattered women gathered outside the corner shop and once downed a blind man by skittling away his stick. He never spoke to us. His house was empty all day. It had little furniture, as we saw when we peered through the windows. Clocks, fiddles and barometers were strewn about and the table was littered with breakfast things, usually including a bowl of porridge he had not had time to finish. In the evening he played the fiddle.

The other white collar resident, our neighbour Mr Halstead, likewise passed us unheeding and dwelt in a house given to music-making. His wife, Madame Smith LRAM, was a teacher of the pianoforte and had a gilt-lettered plaque by the front door to say so. Children arrived for tuition, many of them pale and reserved by nature, others made shy by the humiliation of carrying a music case and wearing their Sunday clothes on week days. They all mastered the first bars of 'An English Country Garden', monotonous at first to us through the wall and then in time a pleasant and reassuring background without which on Sunday evenings my brother and I found it less easy to fall asleep.

Mr Halstead's not speaking to us was different from Mr Riley's. The clock maker lived in another world, of fiddle music and the echoing conundrum of time. Mr Halstead was fully and disagreeably aware of us. He was a fastidious little man, with a well-brushed hat, handkerchief in the top pocket and a rolled umbrella. He ignored us with distaste.

The Halsteads had two children, Dorothea who was about my age, seven, and Bernard who was my brother's age, four. They seldom played out in the street. They were fatter and cleaner and wore different clothes, blazers with yellow piping. This was because they went to a different school, the convent of St Mary, a fee-paying Roman Catholic institution. I began to collect facts about Roman Catholics. I had come across one who taught our class when our regular teacher was off sick. In reading the bible she bowed her head at the name of Jesus and bade us do likewise. 'Well,' my grandfather said, 'she must be a Roman Catholic'. His tone was of surprise but not of disapproval. He said no more. But now we had them on the other side of the wall it could not be left at that. It emerged that we did not know quite what they believed but whatever they believed was wrong. One reason why we did not know was that they did not know themselves. This was partly because proceedings were conducted in Latin which was double dutch to most of them. They believed the priest could forgive sins, which he couldn't; they burned incense, which was meaningless to God and bad for the chest; they had large litters of children and squandered their money on drink. It was obvious that Mr Halstead was neither a fast breeder nor a boozer, but the picture of a Roman Catholic was an abstract which need not accord with fact. Once you got the gist of it you could detect the Roman Catholic quality of things. I thought the bland faces of Mrs Halstead and Dorothea were Catholic faces because of their similarity to those in stained glass windows. I thought for no reason that Bernard's fairy cycle of a slightly unusual design was a Catholic bike. I told people at school that we had Catholics as neighbours, with a sort of pride as one might boast of living next door to a pet shop.

It was a shock to realise that many of the boys I played with on the recreation ground were Catholics and I had always known it. But I then had no notion of what it meant. When Catholicism came to my notice as embodied in the Halsteads it was compounded of pianoforte, social aloofness and blazers with yellow piping. It took an intellectual effort to admit the boys who swarmed about the rec into the same religious category. I put a sharp eye on them when they were not looking in the hope of catching their Catholicism by surprise. There could be no doubt that they belonged. Their school bore the same name as the convent, St Mary's, and was in the same building, although strict apartheid kept the rec boys with their germs and bad language on their own side of a high wall. I realised I had always known about having their sins forgiven. It happened on Saturday mornings. In a football game you never knew when you had them. You would suddenly find yourself down to five men or you would make a back pass under pressure and see to your horror the goal empty and the keeper haring off to the confessional.

It seemed an odd practice. Nonconformists never confessed their sins. They invited other people to confess theirs. When two or three were gathered together they would spend enjoyable hours putting each other in the wrong, ready at any time to forgive opponents if only they would overcome the turpitude of refusing to acknowledge their faults. In theory you could achieve a first-round knock out by sailing straight in and forgiving somebody for something he had not done at all but no paid-up Methodist would go down to a sucker punch like that. They made a day of it. The Catholics on the other hand dispatched sin smartly. They were in and out like the customers of a brisk chip shop. The pace grew hotter as Saturday wore on. Three priests used to arrive breathless on the terraces at Turf Moor only minutes before the kick-off, often when the teams were out on the field. The penitents, we were told, got very short shrift as three o'clock approached. 'Yes, yes, yes,' the priest would say. 'Everybody's at it all the time. Ten Hail Marys. Next.'

The Halsteads were not typical Roman Catholics. Catholics tended to be poorer than the rest. More of them were in labouring jobs or unemployed because, I suppose, of coming from large families and a certain shiftlessness which their church did little to discourage. They did not pay the tremulous attention to illness that we did but they made the most of death. The departed were much recalled in conversation. Our poor Maureen God rest her soul and our Michael who's with the angels were spoken of as though they were expected in for dinner.

Most Roman Catholic families came to Lancashire with the Irish immigrations of the 19th century but they were never an alien minority. The greater part of the population they joined was itself immigrant from one place or another. In no time a common speech developed, shared habits and manners, and less explicably a common physical stature, stocky and sturdy, that made everybody look as though they had all been hatched at one sitting. In Liverpool, whose population was doubled by Irish immigration in a single decade of last century, the Irish influence on speech and behaviour remained. Those who pressed on into the hinterland were assimilated, though in my time most of them still lived in the streets around their church. St Mary's church and Fulledge Wesleyan Methodist chapel more or less fronted each other across Todmorden road. The Catholics lived the other side of the church, we lived our side of the chapel. Nobody was embattled. By 1930 few non-Catholics cared about any kind of church. It was inertia not sectarianism that made families stay put. The arrival in Hinton street of the Halsteads and of Mrs Halstead's older sisters who came to live opposite would have caused no stir. The marks that made them conspicuous and strange were less of their religion than of their social class. They had a bob or two. Very little. Mr Halstead with his umbrella and his squeamish manner turned out to be a clerk at the Co-op.

They never quite fitted in. Both the children were soft, let out to play only occasionally and retrieved when voices rose. One afternoon Mrs Halstead arrived at the door

to complain that my brother Eric had knocked Bernard
unconscious. My mother came back down the passage with
quaking concern. Eric leapt up from his tea. 'Is he bad?' he
said, 'I'll take him my trumpet.' My mother pressed for the
facts. Eric seemed never to have known or to have forgotten
them. She tried to convey the seriousness of what had
happened and reminded him of the grief to his family and
the ruin to himself caused by my grandfather's brother Jim,
a black sheep who carried a pistol. She got nowhere. Then
the door was pounded again and there were Mrs Halstead's
sisters from across the street. They brought a progress report
or, as it turned out, a regress report which they performed
in a dolorous duet. Dear Bernard had fallen into a delirium,
he thought he was at Morecambe. Mr Halstead had been
summoned from his work, the doctor called, the priest sent
for, please God they all came in time. Sinking fast, distraught
and sorrowing mother, wicked act, the beautiful child, self-
same thing as with our Kevin God rest his soul who fell off
a haystack.

My mother in tears pleaded with Eric for an explanation.
Did he not understand what might happen to him? Had he
not heard them say that Bernard was dying? God would
know what had happened. Sins could never be hidden from
him. Faced with the hangman's noose and damnation, Eric
obliged with total recall of the incident, proceeding to such
a profusion of detail that he had to be cut short for elucidation
of the main points. Inconsistencies arose. He first tried to
reconcile them, then swept them aside and generously supplied a totally different account. My mother wept. My
father arrived from work. He was forewarned, having been
accosted in the street by the dolorous sisters who actually
had a priest with them. My father took command. He told
Eric to say what happened and the moment he opened his
mouth caught him by the shirt front like a cowboy menacing
an unobliging bartender. Eric enjoyed an immediate return
of accurate recollection which he expressed in concise choked
sentences. It was clear he was little to blame but my father
dumped him with a bump for the trouble he had caused. He
then washed and changed and called upon Mr Halstead.

My father hated these diplomatic missions but was quite

good at them. He was straightforward, unargumentative
and kept to essentials. His diffidence quietened people's
anger. On this occasion he tactfully omitted the basic fact
that play on the recreation ground was known to be rough.
That was why Bernard was normally forbidden to go
there and also why Eric needed assistance to bring an
unexceptional incident back to mind, which was even more
understandable when it came out that Bernard had walked
home and was only stricken unconscious when he was eating
his teatime custard. My father presented the account he had
elicited. They had been playing leapfrog. Bernard had fallen
under Eric's weight. He cried. They retrieved his specs and
straightened the arm and washed cinders off his face at the
river. They stayed playing there, the accident forgotten.

Mr Halstead withdrew to take counsel with the sisters.
They were now with Mrs Halstead in the front room to the
exclusion of the students of pianoforte who waited in the
passage along with the patient chain-smoking priest. The
sisters' view of the universe was less Roman Catholic than
Manichean. Mr Halstead returned from consulting them
with the insight that Eric, having knocked Bernard over,
must have deliberately ground his face in the cinders because
deposits of them remained deep in his hair and ears. My
father made a measured and placatory reply which the priest
intervened to accept on behalf of his flock. My father
returned home rather pleased with the success of his visit
but when Eric joined in the rejoicing his mood changed.
'Simmer down, lad,' he said. 'Just watch your step.' My
mother protested that that was unfair. If Eric had done
nothing wrong he should not be told to watch his step. 'I'm
talking to both of them,' my father said, including me in his
glare. 'You watch your step too'. My poor mother looked
bewildered. She never got the hang of step watching.

It all fizzled out. Bernard revived. The chain-smoking
priest trudged off to his presbytery. The first notes of 'An
English Country Garden' blossomed from the parlour like
the flowers of a late spring. The dolorous sisters went
back home, the prospects of a darkening night of sorrow
scuppered before nine o'clock. No last rites, no funeral, no
keening, no God rest his soul. Bernard was abroad the

next day, the damaged arm of his spectacles repaired with Elastoplast. He was not allowed to play on the rec again.

The two premises, home and shop, of E.S. Cubbons High Class Boot and Shoe bounded our terrace like a pair of book ends. The window of his shop, at the Lyndhurst road end, carried beside his name two other words in fading gilt, Repairs and Bespoke, which I thought must be a sort of boot polish. Only cripples and people with odd feet still had shoes made to measure. On the glass stands of the window were a dozen pairs of factory-made boots and shoes aimed at old people careless of fashion or incapable of hobbling into town. It must have been a thin trade; the Co-op had already pulled out of bigger and better-equipped local shoe shops Mr Cubbons had a couple of hand-operated machines which would have been welcome to a museum of industrial archaeology (though, come to think of it, there was none and none was needed; the whole of northern England was becoming a museum of industrial archaeology). Mr Cubbons told my father that the shop had belonged to his grandfather and he himself now held on in the hope of better times. 'They'll come,' my father said. 'They must,' said Mr Cubbons. They were both shy sincere men and, although their friendship never developed beyond brief conversations and the exchange of trade journals, they reassured each other. Each believed the other was well placed to notice the first signs of revival in their trade.

It was a surprise to learn that Mr Cubbons was an aficionado of local boxing. It was a low game with a following largely of wizened scarecrows who jeered and growled at the bruisers battling round the small ring. It went on in towns all over the country though the following was small and to make a living the boxers had to take all the fights they could get. Many finished brain-damaged. You saw them shuffling about town in rags unable to recognise people who spoke to them. Pity made a tragedy of decrepitude. He could have been champion of the world if it hadn't been for one thing and another, drink, women, his handlers, gambling – anything except that there were too many fights on the way to the big time and his senses were befuddled before he got there. Even champions finished on their heels.

Mr Cubbons' house at the other end of the row from his shop sheltered his family and a good-natured Labrador called Lady. She was black, a matching accessory for Mrs Cubbons who wore the black cotton of mill workers. Teddy was a school class above me, Douggie was Eric's age. They all had protruding front teeth. Clustered together peeping out from the frame of the small door at the back of the shop window they looked like a family of rabbits. The boys were the first I saw to blow pink balloons of gum which I thought they had some sort of special right to, not only because their oral configuration enabled them to do it well but, vaguely because of the assonance between their family name and bubbly gum. Neither of them played football. Teddy did Meccano, which I understood to be an alternative life style, and instead of riding his bike he tipped it up and took the wheels off. They followed their father's sport. One day they came out in boxing gloves, small boys overbalanced like a pair of deformed insects. Their father, they said, had got the gloves 'trade', no doubt with the double aim of educating them in the noble art and straightening their teeth. They gave an exhibition which confirmed our belief that boxing was a charade of fighting. Our disdain stung. Teddy angrily lisped that he was going in to limber up on the punch ball,

also bought 'trade', and if I would kindly wait he would
return and set about me.

He did not like us. We never responded to him. It was
not only boxing and Meccano that separated us but the great
range of knowledge of interest to Teddy and every intelligent
boy but not to us. He treasured and retailed information
printed across the top of pages in the Wizard about the
number of trees growing in Canada or where all the Boy
Scouts in the world would reach if placed end to end. He
divulged research on the habits of butterflies and he gave up
normal comics for a publication called, I think, Modern
Boy which had as a centre spread a coloured section diagram
to show how a submarine worked. He took our lack of
interest as a rebuff and indeed as a symptom of what irked
him more than the cultural divide. He was older than us,
some part of a year, and had nobody his own age in
neighbouring streets to play with. Our company was unsatis-
factory and beset with the danger that he would be spotted
at play with us by somebody from his own school class.

He hit upon a revenge that neatly embraced all elements
of the problem. He engaged the boys of his class, some
twenty, to come and spoil our football practice on the rec
after school. They made a number of training raids, then
mounted a military operation of great scope and complexity.
One winter Friday afternoon when they were let out of
school early they deployed themselves in groups hidden
round the rec and lay in wait for us. In the failing light they
came first from the side where the river ran, their targets the
ball and the coats we had put down for goal posts. There
were only three of us. As we fought and ran, enemy platoons
rose from behind stone benches, issued from back streets,
and came sliding down coal place roofs. They buffeted and
belted us. They tore up sods from the edges of the rec and
ground the grit into our faces. One lad with his leg in irons
pounded our feet with his heavy heel. We made it to
Norman Clee's front garden in Holmsley street and kicked
the iron gate to. The garden was a strip, little more than a
yard wide, behind a low wall and a privet hedge. They
could easily have broken in. But it was a boundary and they
stopped just as dogs do. Similarly, the front door was a

boundary to us and we would never have thought of taking refuge in the house. We faced them over the privet, leaning out from time to time to dab a punch on anybody who came within range. Norman Clee could outreach most of them. Though younger he was a big boy, but amiable and did not, as they say in the business, punch his weight. The distinctive contribution of our third partner, Kenneth Almond, was to repeat that he would go and get the whip when his dad came home from work and unlocked the house. They brought up siege engines, a pop gun whose cork was restrained by a string, a water pistol which soon clogged with the dirty water from the gutter, and a mop which bobbled our heads round and threated the Clees' front window until we were able to snap the shaft. A wave of revulsion and rage swept the besiegers, an army of Crusaders who had seen the cross shattered. In the ensuing tumult Kenneth Almond had to shout at the top of his voice to make himself heard about bringing the whip. He added when the wave fell back that it was a lion-tamer's whip.

Little had been seen of Teddy Cubbons. His inclination was more to high strategy than to slugging it out, and for a time he disappeared altogether. He returned with the boxing gloves which put new heart into his men. They all had a go, four of them at any one time having a single glove and aiming punches at us above the privet. Then they got fed up of tying and untying the laces. The battle so subsided that when Kenneth Almond's father came home across the street Kenneth was easily able to escape through their ranks and go for his lion-tamer's whip. Teddy's gang drifted away, which was a pity because Mr Almond lighted the gas mantle in the living room at the back of the house and Kenneth returning down the passage threw a grotesque and menacing shadow on the wall in which the whip loomed like the mast of a ship. It turned out to be a penny whip with a lash of shrivelled leather but by then none of the enemy remained to see it except the boy with the two halves of the broken mop shaft who lingered afraid to go home. He was the only one that afternoon to be sure of a real good hiding.

The gang would leave us alone for weeks then molest us every evening. Jack Astin arrived like Shane. He came from

Accrington to live next door to Kenneth Almond. He went
to St Mary's R.C. school so we were denied the normal
preview of his fighting ability in the school yard, but he
inspired confidence. He was older than us, lean and quiet
and with bristly hair like heroes in the Adventure. He had a
big bike which he could lay down like a dirt track rider,
skidding in an arc of cinders and stepping clear as the bike
sank to the ground. He kicked with his left foot which
balanced our game and when his clog spun off he let it lie
and played on in his sock. Some bigger boys, not of Teddy's
gang, stopped for a bit of casual baiting and one eventually
plunged in and kicked our ball over the railings into the
plantation by the river. 'Fetch it,' Jack Astin said. The lad
turned to confront him, hesitated and went for the ball. Jack
said nothing to him on his return. He got on with the game.
When we told him about Teddy's gang he showed no
interest, but when they appeared one evening, howling like
Zulus, he picked up his overcoat by the collar and flayed
into them. He went wild, whirling his coat round his head,
swiping them with buttons and belt buckle, bowling them
over with the sheer force of his charge. Several fled in panic.
The lad with irons on his legs hopped away at an astonishing
speed raising spurts of gravel with his heavy heel. It was
like having a beserk in a mediaeval army. All that was left
for the rest of us was to punch them as they reeled and kick
them when they were down.

Norman Clee was the first to grow his feet big enough to
wear proper football boots. The day he was to appear in
them word spread round the playground and half the boys
of the school came to the rec, an enormous throng jostling
to see as he sat by the railings changing out of his clogs. The
boots were boots, not the excellent slippers of today. The
toecaps were reinforced like those of industrial boots and
polished light brown. The rest of the boot was of undyed
leather and the woven white laces about six yards long. It
was a magnificient sight to see Norman scatter his fans and
bring his boots into play. Football boots soon blackened
and even professionals never came out with them that pale
colour. Small boys ran alongside him. Dogs bounded and

barked. Whenever he stopped he was surrounded. We gave up to trying to play, and the next evening when the voyeurs started to congregate we drove them off with stones and sods.

Football boots, though it was never admitted, were unsuitable for the rec. The top layers of the leather studs were quickly worn away by the cinders and the exposed nails driven up through the sole. Clogs were tactically superior. Their pointed toe bruised deeper and those fastened by clasps often flew off into the faces of opponents. Those of us who had neither football boots nor clogs were obliged to develop a certain immunity to pain and to compensate by greater ferocity or meanness.

It did not strike us as unfair that Norman alone should have a pair of football boots. Besides having big feet, he came from the big time. His home was a centre of glamour. His beautiful cousin lived there, an attendant at the Pentridge pictures, and she was called for by a young professional footballer. Both spoke to us without condescension as though they were ordinary people. But of course they weren't. The smell of the Pentridge lingered round her, the scent of the spray she pumped into the air between houses to grapple with the germs and smells the departing audience left behind. We took it that she was part of the life of the silver screen, one of the actresses come down amongst us, so to speak, whose photograph would soon be in the gallery of stills in the foyer where she tore the tickets. She wore posh clothes on weekdays and so did he. They were free at hours when ordinary people were at work. They were modest. He changed the subject if you said anything about last Saturday's game. She confessed she did not know Buck Jones.

Norman's father sat there unnoticed, partly because he was always there and partly because he hardly existed. He was unemployed which was a misfortune that eventually became an identity. I do not suppose he was forty but he seemed very old with a pale bald head and a waistcoat that was never buttoned. He drank tea all day. The table was covered with newspaper ringed by the sticky base of the tin from which he dangled condensed milk into his pint pot.

He smoked cigarettes a bit at a time, putting them out in a shower of sparks and lighting butts so short that his eyebrows were permanently singed. He seldom spoke. Norman's mother did the dialogue. She had a strong contralto voice that carried as far as the rec when she called Norman from their yard. She pampered him with double helpings of condensed milk spooned into his tea and called him by a pet name, Chicken, which she sang out from the back door, to his shame, our embarrassment and the glee of our enemies.

Because of his size he got the bear's part in the Christmas concert at school. We presented 'Ten Little Nigger Boys' which required us to black up with soot and Norman to wear a bear's head. It did not arrive. The teacher told him to bring the hearthrug from home to resemble a pelt and to make little eyes. The rug was useless for the purpose, completely threadbare, so that when Norman came on, peering through half-closed eyes, he looked less like a bear than a son of the desert down on his luck. Laughter almost drowned the piano and the singing.

> Three little nigger boys going round the zoo,
> A big bear hugged one and then there were two.

Norman's embrace of a sooty child sprang the safety pin holding his rug. It fell to a howl that might have greeted a stripper's drawers. The Cubbins mob started to chant 'Chicken'. On the way home, still blacked up, we fought a running battle with them the length of Lyndhurst road. It was an unexpected variation on the theme of Christmas to residents who peered round the curtains and the nearest Burnley ever came to staging a race riot.

The Benns lived a few doors away from Norman in Holmsley street. They were a distinctive family coming from away and I felt it distinguished us to be their first friends. Mrs Benns was sitting on a bench in Towneley park with her infant son Arnold when my mother with Eric spoke to her. It was the first social conversation she had had since they arrived in Burnley and she was overcome. She came to tea wearing gilt-framed glasses which in my supposition that everything was peculiar to its place of origin I assumed to be Yarmouth specs. Arnold wore an angora frock or jersey with kittens round the hem. I remember a rather defensive surprise among our neighbours at her complaint of loneliness. People in the cotton towns were unaware of their brusque manners and expected their friendliness to be taken for granted. There was no place for the overtures and responses of growing acquaintance. My grandmother understood. She also had come from a gentler place, though not nearly so far away, and the manners and speech of East Lancashire still seemed rough and lacking in formal courtesies. It must have been like arriving late at a party where all the other guests know each other and are already half drunk.

Loneliness did not worry Arthur Benns. He tramped the moors alone and listened alone to classical music played on gramophone records. He took no interest in anything else. Although he was a cabinet maker their home was bare. There was a magnificient hallstand he had made at the end of his apprenticeship, though nothing much to hang on it, and a good cabinet to house his gramophone. Beyond that there were only a few sticks of cheap furniture, some of it broken in minor ways. They had no carpets. The house smelled of carbolic soap. A barometer arrived, the gift of Mr Riley the clockmaker who was the one man in the district after Arthur's heart. It remained the only embellishment in the room. Perhaps they hoped he would some day come up with a clock. In the meantime they had an alarm clock, which would only go when placed on its face.

Arthur Benns had receding hair and high cheek bones which gave him an intellectual, rather Slavonic appearance. He lay back, eyes closed, listening to records. When one ended he would reach out with long arms to light a paper spill at the fire for his pipe or to turn up the clock. He acquired an organ from somewhere and played it with such abandon that the floorboards vibrated the length of the terrace. He had opinions but did not discuss them. He was an atheist because his mother had died in pain. He was also a socialist because he thought capitalism 'a blooming daft carry-on'.

And indeed it was. When his old boss in Norfolk went

out of business Arthur had to shift 200 miles to Lancashire to get any work at all. He landed at the cabinet making factory where my uncle Ben worked, knocking up volumes of cheap furniture at piece rates. They alternated between working like demons and doing nothing, slogging along until the shops and warehouses were full, then going on the dole. There were few power tools and little need for them. Human energy was cheap; a reserve supply of it queued every morning outside the works door. They were pallid men, the cabinet makers, the colour of wood. They were all on the look-out for a place where coffins were made. That was a steady job, booming at Christmas in preparation for the winter rush, and certain minimum standards had to be maintained. You could market dressing tables that collapsed but not coffins that let the corpse through the bottom.

What most saddened tradesmen was that the skill on which their pride and identity depended was no longer valued or of much use. Factories were at an unhappy mid-stage between craft work and the production line. Skilled men were miscast to achieve a result that later was better achieved by machines and organisation. The hardest thing to swallow was that lower standards were expected and accepted. Arthur Benns was amazed to see the foreman pass without comment a man who was giving screws a good start with the hammer. 'If that's what they blooming well want that's what I'll do,' he said. But he didn't. They had a conscience about the customer and a pride to protect that was badly enough wounded already.

They kept their pecker up with practical jokes. Arthur Benns, new and eccentric, was an ideal victim. His mates worked up to impregnating the tobacco in the bowl of his pipe with paraffin which went up with an explosion that lighted the shop and frizzled what remained of his quiff. He took it well. It was not in his nature either to complain or to retaliate. When he went down ill his workmates arrived in the evening bringing a bagful of the offcuts of wood they were allowed to take for the fire and staying to sit with him. He had rheumatic fever, a dangerous illness that caused torment when he moved his limbs. Like any long-term invalid he had to be brought down to the warmth of the living room. It meant shifting him on to the floor, getting the bed down in pieces then humping him down after it. Both uncle Ben and my father were good at humping but of rather different loads. Uncle Ben had practised on sideboards and my father on ammunition boxes. Poor Arthur howled. Uncle Ben came back pale and my father red. The clock-maker had promised a comforting rendition on the fiddle and we faintly heard him starting up. Neither uncle Ben nor my father said anything but they plainly thought the howling and the fiddling the rum sort of carry-on that happened when people moved in from foreign parts.

The illness reduced the Benns family to destitution. They were still paying off for their removal from Great Yarmouth and for some reason Arthur either did not qualify for sickness pay or only for a low rate. Mrs Benns' mother, an apple of a woman from Norfolk, came up but her help was of limited value. She had a weak heart which made it necessary to rest much of the time and she was broke, having spent all her money on an ominously one-way ticket. People gave them what they could. We would sit down to tea and find the jam had gone. Loaves got lopped in half, a plate of tripe in the pantry disappeared from beneath our very noses, the salad was waylaid on its way to the Sunday tea. We were not allowed any joking comment or even to inquire whether Mrs Benns had been. Arthur's workmates had a whip-round for him, auntie Abbie landed with a basketful of food bought on tick, Jack Yates sent him some socialist pamphlets, Arnold increasingly ate with us. At their home the gas mantle was lighted only in the evening when visitors were due and turned down to a dismal level when they had gone. They were completely cleaned out. Arthur declined, and so did Mrs Benns' mother. As they lay in the dark bare room it seemed only a question of who would go first.

At this low ebb the vicar pounced. Mrs Benns was a practising communicant of the Church of England. She observed all the feasts and baked a saffron loaf at Easter. The vicar asked Arthur while time remained to recant the atheism brought on by his mother's painful death. Arthur replied that his own suffering only fortified his lack of belief.

That, the vicar argued was illogical; Arthur's resentment about the way they had been put through it necessarily implied, did it not, an author of the suffering? On that evidence considered alone it might be concluded that God was malevolent but it would be contradictory to conclude that he did not exist. I ache therefore he is. Arthur dulled by the pain of his racked limbs did not completely grasp the argument but he caught the drift and it stung him to a reply that brought Mrs Benns and her mother to tears. 'That's blooming daft,' he said. 'Buzz off and shut the gate.'

Across Holmsley street from the Benns, on the same side as Kenneth Almond and Jack Astin, lived a girl called Jenny who sometimes played football with us. Several girls applied to play but they proved frivolous and threatened to bring the game into disrepute. Jenny moved and kicked like a footballer. You did not even notice she was a girl unless ribald passers-by called attention. One afternoon she started to weep, in public, on the open rec, under the blank gaze of a hundred windows. She sobbed something about her father and broke away. She was so upset that she ran off not in the style of a footballer but splaying out her clogs like women running late to the mill or Minnie Mouse.

We speculated about what might have happened to her father. Jack Astin had heard of somebody who had been carried round by an overhead belt and killed. Kenneth Almond said he hadn't been killed because he had seen him half an hour ago sitting by the fire. It was the wrong time to be sitting by the fire and I remembered my father in the armchair the afternoon he got the needles of the stitching machine through his hand. Kenneth Almond said there were no stitching machines where Jenny's father worked. Allowing imagination full rein we surmised there might be other apparatus besides endless belts and stitching machines capable of putting toilers in the armchair. Kenneth Almond said Jenny's father was sitting, as my father had sat, 'doing nowt and saying nowt'. But he was not injured, Kenneth discovered next day. There had been a 'misunderstanding'. We did not know what that meant, but we gathered it was in some way a disgrace. We hoped that he might have held up a bank and was waiting to be arrested, but we really knew it was not of that order. We divined that it was the kind of offence of which we knew only vaguely through oblique references between adults and conversations which stopped when we came into the room.

It came to light that Jenny's father had not been going to work. He had left home with his bait box at half past six in the morning and returned at five in the afternoon but he had spent the day in secret places. He was caught taking the shoe brushes with him, a curious incident which he curtly managed to pass off, then he was spotted by a neighbour. Her innocent curiosity led to his downfall. He confessed that he had not been to work. On fine days he had gone country walks on the other side of town. When it rained he had whiled away the hours in the library, not in the reading room which steamed up like a laundry from the throng of men but in the reference library which was always so empty you could hear the clock bump the minutes. It was there against all odds that the neighbour spotted him. He made a full confession and apologised for having been cross in the incident about the boot brushes which he had needed to get rid of traces of his country hikes. His family pressed him to say what had put him off his job. He confessed that he had no job. He had been played off. He was on the dole. His scheme of deception was devised to conceal his idleness. Jenny did not come to play for several weeks after he was found out.

15 · GAMES

Normally girls did not join in our play. They played their games and we played ours. We shared the street without quarrelling. The paving stones they chalked for hopscotch, the railings to which they fastened their skipping ropes, and the lamp-post on which we chalked our wickets were established by custom. Mobile games, bike races, gun battles, taking dolls in prams shopping, were played in among the fixed pitches. Deliberate spoiling of somebody's game was rare and clamorously condemned. Accidental collisions were frequent. The right of rebuke belonged to girls alone. They caricatured the exasperation of women mill workers telling off the tackler. 'You are a pain, lad. Why don't you watch where you're going?' Eric's cowboy hat was outlawed. It had a soft crown of such depth that the cardboard brim fell over his eyes. His blind charge with his pistol brought him down in a tangle of children, dogs, skipping ropes, prams and bikes. He was roughed up by girls who then rounded on Douggie Cubbons who had no hat but was carrying a six-shooter. 'Don't wear your hat,' he lisped to Eric next time. 'It geth uth i' lumber. We'll hath thum grub.'

His grub was a bagful of gritty fawn lozenges his mother threw out when she stopped coughing. Their part in the Wild West was to serve as an elixir. Anyone shot would be revived with grub from Douggie's bag. Sheriffs, bad-hats, posses, tribes of Indians and squadrons of U.S. Cavalry arrived from streets around and died without argument. Hinton street looked like the marshalling yard at Atlanta with Douggie Cubbons crawling among the wounded, breaking off smaller and smaller pieces of his dwindling supply of cough tablets and saying to each croaking warrior, 'Reckon I give you thum grub and you geth bether'. The dead arose with their weapons. It was sacrament, resurrection and Valhalla all in one.

Such novelties were memorable because they were rare. It was not cough sweets we lacked so much as imagination. Most of our games were formless and repetitive. My father as a boy had played marbles in many forms. We played it along the gutter in only one form; you aimed at your opponent's marble, then it was his turn to aim at yours. What you hit you won. The only elaboration was not in the form of the game but in a set of rather mean rules. All marbles we called bobbers. You aimed with a large ball bearing called an ironie which, before your opponent's turn, you substituted with the smallest glass bobber, which you then trod into the sludge, leaving only a glint visible. Whether the aimed bobber had glanced such a small target was almost impossible to judge and was resolved by argument and often fighting between the contestants and their supporters in the gangs of boys who followed games like spectators round a roulette table. The players usually resumed after fighting. If your bobber was hit you could either give it up or open a credit account with your opponent. The little glassies put down as a target counted one. At the end of play the loser could pay in oners or in bigger bobbers worth more. The ironies were worth twelve. It did sometimes happen that a player skint of all his bobbers finally lost his ironie. Such boys were spoken of with a sense of awe and folly as gamblers who have lost their businesses at the tables are pointed out in casinos.

There were endless wrangles about the rating of the bobbers. The glass ones with a marbled finish did not exactly correspond in size or value to those in plain glass with a filament of colour. My big stone bobber bought when we lived at the other side of town was banned as foreign currency. Nobody would play for taws, pellets of coloured clay whose only use was for aunts to buy and small children to swallow. A boy who was discovered playing with a marble broken out from the neck of a pop bottle and coloured with chalks was nearly lynched. You could gain advantages by shouting first. If your bobber lodged behind a screen of garbage you had to shout 'No shifts' before he shouted 'Shifts'. If it stopped hard against the kerb you shouted 'No pea rolls', to prevent him from rolling his ironie along the guiding angle of the gutter. It was all contention. Marauders broke into the groups to make the best of the opportunity to kick bending boys. Most adopted the practice sparingly to equalize with their enemies. Others took it up full time and kicked bobber players at random. I cannot remember what months the bobber season occupied but I remember sludgy gutters and numb fingers so I suppose it was autumn or winter. It ended when all the bobbers had gone down the grates. A boy was always posted to guard off the grate with his splayed out clogs but the bobbers often went between his heels and drowned with a deep soulful plop. Grates that had swallowed somebody's ironie were pointed out like the site of an industrial disaster.

In the school yard we played chasing games and fighting. Football with a ball was banned but some of the teachers on yard patrol would permit dribbling with a piece of coke from the caretaker's heap. The teacher from the top class bore the trial of yard duty by putting himself into a trance and moving glassy-eyed through the swirl and scuffle of boys until he was snapped out by the bell or by children colliding with him or by a serious fight. Wrestling and throwing people was all right, but punching, keeping somebody down or banging heads on the ground was not. A serious flare-up brought the whole playground in seconds to a hooting scrum round the fighters. The teacher waded in, spitting hatred, collared the contestants and marched them in to the headmaster who assaulted both of them as a lesson against violence.

Girls in their own yard shut off from ours by a locked iron gate had a season of performing handstands against the wall which the headmaster recognized as a harmless activity but one to be confined to parts of the yard concealed from the public gaze lest it seem indecorous to elderly passers-by.

Crazes came and went in games which had some mileage in them like yoyos and top and whip but also in things whose amusement you would not have expected to last for a day. For weeks hundreds of children went round behind swelling and collapsing balloons of bubbly gum as though a frightful epidemic had blighted their faces. We bought penny tin frogs mounted on a tension plate which clicked when it was pressed and clacked when it was released. If you set the frog down with the plate compressed it would leap a few inches. We went round clicking and clacking at each other. If there had been school psychologists they would no doubt have divined meanings. People who clacked their frog in school were not analysed but caned. Those whose frog accidentally went off in their pocket or who inadvertently sat on it were also caned. Thus this rather limited toy became an object of suspense and danger as though it was a venomous snake we all carried round.

Crazes took a week or two to develop. You could not just go and buy a frog because people were click-clacking about. You would have to wait for your Friday penny and if you only got a halfpenny you would have to wait for two Fridays, going sweetless the while. Even if you had the money it was not a thing to rush into. You might invest all your gold only to find that this time the craze did not catch on and you would be left with a brand new frog smelling sweetly of fresh paint which you would be ridiculed for click-clacking out of season. What was then despised was not only the practice but the thing itself. 'Ar, he's got a bloody frog', boys would sneer who themselves only months before had clacked their frog flaccid and voiceless.

Craze seasons were moveable feasts. Their advent was uncertain and their duration incalculable. They rose and sank in a swell of popular interest, nobody knew why. I suppose there may have been specific advertising of yoyos and bubbly gum but it was nothing compared to modern campaigns. Nobody promoted frogs and certainly nobody promoted tops and whips which girls played with all the year round. For boys tops was a craze of limited duration which needed to be strictly observed to avoid the double contempt of playing a game which was out of season and, being out of season, a girl's game. Having limited practice, we never rivalled the skill of girls who could drive a top the length of the street pavement and back. We tried to cut a dash by buying 'window-breakers', tops which were not conical in section but T-shaped. They were highly unstable and hard to get started but once under way could be lashed into high arcs which menaced the hoods of prams and the heads of tricyclists. Some girls, usually little fat ones, had squat jumbo tops which were easy to start with a twirl of the fingers but needed a good eye and hand to lash. The ample surface of the jumbos was good for chalking coloured patterns which changed with the speed of rotation. Girls did most things better. They were good with the biffbat, sharply repelling the ball that scutched back at them on a length of elastic. They could fling yoyos in all directions. A few could even play diabolo. The diabolo was a wooden object like two cones joined at their point, in section like a bow tie. The narrow part was placed over a length of string which the player controlled with two handles, raising each side alternately until the diabolo, spinning on the tautened string, could be propelled with an opening of the arms into the air and caught again on the string. To master it required patience and freedom from marauders which girls enjoyed and boys did not. They developed intricate routines of clapping and twirling and jumping in time with the bounce of a ball between hands and pavement and wall and to the metre of a rhyme:

Nebuchadnezzar the king of the Jews sold his wife for a pair of shoes,
When the shoes began to wear, Nebuchadnezzar began to swear,
When the swearing began to stop, Nebuchadnezzar bought a shop,
When the shop began to sell, Nebuchadnezzar bought a bell,
When the bell began to ring, Nebuchadnezzar began to sing . . .

We played hide and seek together. Both boys and girls played with hoops of plywood or, better, of iron which rumbled resonantly over the joins in the pavement and brought people to the door clutching their heads. Boys alone had motor tyres which were thought unladylike. They were directionally unstable and liable at speed to cut swathes through smaller children and to strike and splatter with the water that collected inside the case adults not sprightly enough to leap out of their path. The tyre became a first strike weapon. The wooden hoop became with boys a quoit to aim at the arm of gas lamps, the iron hoop a clamp to manacle small children to the railings. Girls persisted in the proper purpose. In this and other street games they developed the skill to make their pleasures last. They did their own things better and one girl at Todmorden road school did our things better too. She could beat us at bobbers and she could fight us. She cleaned us out and she panned us out on the pavement, sitting on our chest and stretching our arms out alongside our ears. We yearned for sex equality many years before kind ladies took up our cause.

Our domain was the recreation ground. It lay at the end of the street where the town ended, a surprise of open space, as welcome as the sight of the ocean to an explorer emerging from dark forests. It was a plain of cinders bounded on the far side by a shallow river. Beyond lay the parkland of Towneley Holmes and beyond again the moorland hills criss-crossed by walls and dotted with farms. On fine summer mornings you could sometimes hear a farm dog bark so far away it sounded like a memory. The open aspect enhanced the feeling of freedom and release. The rec belonged to us. Girls and small children were confined to playing round the boundary among the sweet-smelling weeds. Parents usually stopped short at the railings.

What we did on the rec, practising football and cricket, we did with a dogged persistance equal to what girls brought to their street games and far beyond what most of us were able ever again to summon up for the tasks of life. We spent the school holidays on the rec and every fine evening after school. We called home for a jam butty and the ball and played until in winter all the gas lamps were lighted along the boundary streets and the ball came up like a leap of solidifying darkness. Sometimes our gritty football hurtling out of the night floored passers-by, adults who took short

cuts across the rec, and we would judge from their demeanour as they rose to hands and knees whether to apologise or
to run.

Men sometimes joined in. The worst dribbled our ball
away and tormented us by passing it round and over us.
When we did get a foot on it they would lift us off in
shocking violation of the rules of the game. Others sidled
up longing for a kick and when the ball bounced to them
edged into the game. You could not depend on them. Some
would light up and play with a fag in. Others if spotted by
their friends would pretend they were not really playing and
might even go so far in treachery as to make jocular remarks
about our ball, which was rarely a proper football, or our
persons. But some came and organised full-scale matches,
men of easy humour, usually unemployed coal miners whose
itch to play was as strong as ours. They picked up balanced
sides at the beginning and they reorganised them without
stopping the game as team strengths varied between six and
thirty with new arrivals and the departure of footballers
summoned home through the railings, detached by passing
bands of friends or maimed. You could not play on the rec
what was called a 'brainy game'. You either sailed in or you
did not play. We bounced off the colliers as though we had
hit gate posts. One evening I was knocked dateless with the
ball. The young man who had kicked it left the game,
which I remember thinking was very good of him, and
delivered me to my grandmother who was alone in the
house. My head throbbed and my ear sang. When he left I
wept. My grandmother asked how I would manage when I
was a professional footballer if I wept when I was hit by the
ball. She gave me the story of Joseph to read not because it
was apposite but because it was the only story book she
could find, made me a cup of tea and sat opposite me. The
gas light sang and the burning in my ear subsided. Once
when I looked up she spoke gently about pain and purpose,
of giving and not counting the cost, of fighting and not
heeding the wounds. It was an evening of great serenity and
I was sorry to hear the door open and other people coming
into the house.

It occurs to me that I have written little about my

grandmother. She was a self-effacing person, around whom incidents did not arise. She did not speak much and indeed in the presence of my grandfather got little opportunity, but it was she whose advice I usually sought. She treated a child's perplexities seriously. Her comments were brief and modestly offered but they often threw light on an area much larger than the one to which they were addressed. They illuminated my childhood as the lives of older people have been enlightened by the sayings of Dr Johnson or the thoughts of Pascal.

Sunday School League matches were played on the rec on Saturday afternoons, watched by a few old men, mocked by the roar from Turf Moor less than half a mile away. The real contests were in the evenings of early spring when works teams competed for the Hospital Cup. The matches were played every week night on recs all over Burnley so there was little time for passions to cool or for the combatants to recuperate from their wounds. The finalists reached their great night at Turf Moor with a team of crocks. Indeed before it was explained to me that the Hospital Cup was for charity I fancied it was so named because of the large number of injured it sent to the wards. Out of training as most were, the players pulled their muscles, tore their ligaments and went down like felled trees.

The happy pattern Marx perceived in the affairs of men of tragedy succeeded by farce was here reversed. The teams came rumbling out of the wooden changing hut more like a penurious troop of circus performers than a football team. They seldom had a full set of jerseys and never matching shorts or socks. Some wore a cloth cap turned backwards like George Formby on his motor bike. Usually at least one came without kit and trotted out with his trousers tucked down his socks. Half of them smoked while they were kicking in. Women with push chairs and loose children sauntered on the pitch and talked to them. The game started. The ball bobbled in a flurry of grunts and curses. Sometimes, particularly with teams that had no chance, affable players and supporters kept the farce going for the whole of the match. More often bitterness shrivelled everybody's soul from the moment of the referee's first decision. Old men quavered, women shrieked. Just as the footballers were not proper footballers, the spectators were not proper spectators. They lacked the vocabulary, the ritualistic responses, the phasing and the orchestration of practised barracking. They shouted things people might say in a domestic row. When a player was injured his relatives broke ranks and poured on to the pitch, drawing with them team officials, people eager to demonstrate their first-aid training, dogs, busybodies and persons of feeble mind. The felled player would be told not to move, doubled up, massaged, embrocated and dosed from flasks and bottles while a wife or sister plaintively recited his medical history and bemoaned the imprudence of playing football. Meanwhile the stretcher would have been dislodged from the cross beams of the hut, and the player would be carried off. Even if wholly conscious he was expected to close his eyes. Quite often he was restored by a smoke in the hut and came back to a great cheer. More stubborn cases were collected by an ambulance which with no sense of propriety was driven over the pitch, cancelling the game with tyre marks across the scuffed cinders. Spectators and players, some still in their jerseys, stood around in groups long after dark reluctant to let the happening pass.

I do remember one player put back on his feet in an instant. He went down with a thigh strain which was treated with Sloan's Liniment. They applied it with such vigour that in massaging his thigh they accidentally massaged his balls as well. He thrashed clear and charged round in agony bellowing like an enraged bull. Waves of merriment spread through the crowd, renewed afterwards whenever he joined in the action. They left in good humour as I imagine people went home after a bear-baiting.

Cinders make an ideal surface for a recreation ground in daily use. The grass playing fields which took their place are too sloppy in winter for good football and too bumpy in summer for good cricket. A football plays true off cinders and a cricket ball fairly true. They drain well. We were seldom unable to play because of wet. It is a coarse surface to fall on – rec footballers have blue weals on their knees

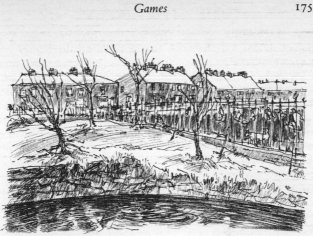

which last a lifetime – but cricket balls seldom bounce high enough to soften the head. The worst thing was to be hit by a cricket ball from another game; surprise and shock made the pain at best excruciating and at worst dull and vaguely located as though it might explode and bring your last moment.

Football ended and cricket began with the suddenness of spring on the Prairie. One day everybody was playing football, the next cricket. Such overlap as happened was caused by the kind of smaller children who turned up an hour late at school when the clocks were put forward. On Saturday mornings, Easter gone, the amplitude of the weekend stretched ahead and beyond that the promise of a lifetime of summer Saturdays. The horse-drawn milk vans from the Co-op dairy returned from different parts of the town towards midday. When they reached Mitella street which bounded the rec on one side the horses nearing home began to trot. They passed in procession like a noontime frieze, and near and far mill buzzers sounded the last post to the working week. For an hour the rec lay empty and the whole town still. Then the first of the afternoon's cricketers arrived with boxes, leisurely and amiable, brilliantined and wearing sports coats. Old men who had no special clothes

for Saturday passed the other side of the railings on their
way to the Lancashire League match at Turf Moor. Women
with push chairs and children and carrier bags filled with
picnic food crossed the rec towards the open country anxious
about the practice balls which rose round the perimeter.
You felt the warmth of the sun and caught the tang of the
moors on the wind. The town was silent. We did not stay
to watch the matches but their beginning, tossing the coin,
setting the field, taking middle, was an overture to the
spacious Saturday afternoons of summer.

On weekdays we practised cricket after tea, not before,
because it could not be abandoned as easily as football. Once
you had had your innings you were under obligation to stay
and give everybody else their's. Wretched boys whose
mother persisted in shouting for them would plead to be
allowed away and sometimes in desperation make a dash for
it. Insults and cinders were thrown after them but it was a
fairly common offence and they came back after a day or
two. We knew who were the honourable people who would
let their mother bleat herself hoarse rather than do you out
of your innings and who were fickle. They were usually
made to bat last.

We played with hard cork balls bought at Woolworths
for sixpence. They lasted a whole season on the cinders
before they began to disintegrate and kept their shape better
than old leather cricket balls. Most of our bats were full-
sized ones with half of the blade sawn off, the sort of thing
you might see a comic dwarf ambling along with. But they
had sprung handles which prevented the impact of the ball
on the blade from stinging the hands. The springing was
insulation, strips of rubber inserted into the handle. You
could see the top edge of them. The sawn down bats had
three rubber strips. They were three-springers. Bats of boys'
size, perhaps because of the thinner handle, were two-
springers which was just about satisfactory, but some were
one-springers or without springing which was no good at
all. A lot of rubbish was sold in those days and cheating on
quality so widespread that few shops would stand by the
manufactured goods they retailed. I saved up for a bat for
God knows how long which when it was new everyone

borrowed for his innings but only once. It stung. Some
boys flung it away and wrung their hands. I refused to
admit it stung. It was a two-springer. You could see the end
of the inserts of red rubber in the top of the handle. It could
not sting unless you got the ball right at the bottom where
any bat stung. My grandfather prescribed linseed oil and
showed me how to bind the blade with string, which I
suppose is intended to prevent the deepening of cracks rather
than to provide insulation. I acquired an immunity to
stinging like an electrician to shocks. Near the end of the
season the string binding the handle began to unwind. It
revealed rubber springs which anyone would suppose ran
the length of the handle. They were not half an inch deep. I
did not divulge this. I did not want to admit I had been
wrong, and I began to feel towards the bat which I had
defended all summer a special companionship and solicitude
such as one might feel for a dog that turns out to be lame.

Demon bowling came to the rec. It was an aspect of the
game which would shortly reach its full glory in Harold
Larwood who brained half the Australian cricket team and
nearly brought down the empire. It was not really suited to
the congestion of the rec. There were no boundaries. Sunday
School League players had to run them all. A snick off a fast
ball could travel so far that the batsmen ran up an astro-
nomical score while fielders fought their way through other
games or teetered on stepping stones to retrieve the ball
from the river. I once saw a fourteener run. Games were
easily lost by fast bowlers or so stretched out that night fell.
They prided themselves on taking immense runs. One went
so far back you lost him in among the other matches. You
would see his plume of dust, then he would appear skittling
over cyclists and women with prams, sending dogs and
children rolling in the dirt, whipping past the wicket-keeper
of another match and finally letting go a delivery which
might fly anywhere. He uprooted wickets, he laid out
batsmen, wicket-keepers, pipe-smoking strollers and square
leg umpires, and one evening his outswinger flew straight
through the downstairs window of a house which overlooked the rec. The family sat with their irons poised over
their steaming suppers, all looking towards the hole in the

glass as though they expected to be photographed. Few of the inhabitants were transfixed in this manner. Perhaps by a process of natural selection the houses overlooking the rec came to be occupied by ferrety little men who shot out like greyhounds from a trap at the first crash of glass. They were mentally flexible as well, ready equally to accept apologies and negotiate compensation with those who stood their ground or to pursue and batter those who ran. 'Only the scum run when they bust a window,' the lads said.

The rec was run by precept and custom. We played at our own spot just as girls did in the streets. We would have had a sense of trespass if we had gone anywhere else or if we had arrived to find somebody on our practice patch. Either way nothing would be said. Custom is not upheld by dispute. Playing round the perimeter we knew exactly where we were by street ends and lamp posts, but Sunday School League cricketers who played out in the middle were equally sure at finding their own spot. They ambled out and pitched their wickets as unerringly as though they incorporated inertial navigation systems in their cloth caps. When they were the away team they might still play on our rec but on their opponents' pitch, which some batsmen said disorientated them more than playing on a different rec.

Among boys there were accepted rules governing visits by the relations of other boys. If somebody's mother or older sister came, especially if she arrived in apron and slippers, you spared his humiliation by pretending not to notice. If a younger brother or sister arrived you joined him in telling them to bugger off. If his dog came you had to say it was a grand dog and not to be annoyed while it bounded about the pitch and slobbered on the ball. If his father or grandfather came you let him do well and called him by his Christian name rather than his nickname, which often sounded odd.

There were actually by-laws governing the use of the rec, signed by a past town clerk and of such amplitude that they filled large display boards in small print. Nobody ever read them. Their spirit was no doubt summed up by the large words on other boards: 'No stone throwing. No betting. Commit no nuisance.' There was a rec keeper, distinguished

by a peak cap. He was not a groundsman – a rec needs none
– and he was more than an official; he was an officer. He did
not speak to boys. He did not interfere. There was no
conflict. The best of the by-laws, I suppose, had been
absorbed into custom and the rest forgotten. He kept to a
stone hut on the Mitella street side of the rec from which he
emerged in spring as though from hibernation. He was a
squat old man who so well fitted the squat door that it
seemed the hut had been especially built to house him. We
never saw him come and go and it was a shock to learn that
he did not live there but in a house in Holmsley street. He
was further said to be somebody's grandfather, which was
hard to reconcile with his remoteness. Being a family man
was at odds with his authority. The commanding figures in
our mythology, Jesus, Richard the Lionheart, Dr Living-
stone and Buffalo Bill, were all loners. But they had cronies
and so did he. In winter they sat coughing with him behind
the closed door of the hut. In summer they sat impassively,
four of them, on a stone bench outside. One died. They left a
gap where he had sat on the bench and the three who remained
looked like an old man's jaw with a tooth missing. Batsmen
said they would cut one through the gap but nobody every
did, out of respect for authority.

On Sundays nobody played on the rec out of respect for
God. Not quite, I suppose. Out of respect for observation
of the Sabbath, out of respect for those who wished the
Sabbath to be observed but as in everything out of respect
for custom. There may well have been among the by-laws
one prohibiting the use of the rec on Sunday. If so it was
superfluous. The prohibition of custom was absolute. You
would sometimes see two or three children in their best
clothes playing on the rec on Sunday. They would almost
certainly be visitors to a household without children of its
own and ignorant of practice. Nobody bothered. It just
seemed odd. Regular users of the rec accepted its non-use
on Sunday without thought and without resentment. Those
who loved the rec enjoyed its different mood on Sunday,
still, its great expanse enhanced by the few small figures
walking across it, and at rest.

One night there was a cloud burst and for several days the

rec lay under water. It was like the fulfilment of a promise. The streets that ran to the boundary always had something of the spaciousness of streets that run to the sea. Now the sea had arrived. People came to promenade on Thursfield road, dogs barked at floating sticks. We raced to the front door each morning and home from school in the afternoon to make sure the sea was still there. Small children brought buckets and spades and waited for the tide to go out. A bigger boy said it would be fathoms deep in the middle and he intended to cross in a boat to which he had access through a friend of his uncle's who worked on the boats at Thompson park whence it would be carried on people's heads in accordance with the practice on safari. The flood was bringing out a new kind of denizen to the rec as flash floods in Australia give a brief life to creatures unseen through the dry years. Our flood like their's disappeared as quickly as it came. One day the lake retreated into separate pools, the next all that remained was a tacky silt over the areas last to drain. My grandmother said that after the Flood which Noah survived God promised that he would never again flood the world and the rainbow was the token of that promise. My grandfather read out an item from the paper about the volume of sewage regurgitated by the flooding of the pipes.

16 · STANLEY'S WORLD

Auntie Abbie's house half a mile away in Irene street had a richer and more mellow quality than ours. It was created in part by the more valuable pieces of furniture that had belonged to the grandparents, the organ which they gave her on marriage and the secretaire and wall clock which remained from the sale of their home; in part by auntie Abbie's liking for good living which propelled her towards an opulence that shocked my mother; and in part by the gentler, more sedentary and studious life of our cousins Stanley and Margaret. Our own home usually felt warm and welcoming; when we returned from the Kerrys it was like going back to barracks.

Stanley spent his time with books and paints and modelling clay, and a collection of his works was on permanent exhibition about the house. He did not go about with gangs of boys or play ball games. The sight of one eye had always been poor; a severe illness at the age of six confirmed him in gentler pastimes. The illness was scarlet fever which was epidemic through the schools every winter. Dr Dixon despaired of Stanley's life. We were not allowed to visit for fear of infection. My grandfather took me as close as the far end of the street and told me to wait there. I saw him admitted and heard the door close behind him. It was late Saturday afternoon after a reserve football match. The gas lamps had come on and the melted snow in ruts and puddles on the unpaved street was beginning to freeze again. I was able for the first time to imagine Stanley not laughing and jolly but lying without his spectacles on the point of death.

Nobody was about in the street. Its cold and desolation sank into memory for most of a lifetime and came back like a fulfilled premonition when he died a few years ago.

We learned then of cares he had long concealed in a life which had seemed to be of endless jollity. Even as a boy he was reticent and it was a surprise to his parents when in the delirium of illness fear of his schoolteachers came to the surface. His conduct and progress were exemplary. He was never in trouble. The teachers favoured him. What frightened him, it emerged, was their manner and appearance, strange old creatures in the gloomy classrooms of Fulledge school. They were the last of their kind, perhaps in youth not blessed with beauty and socially isolated by their profession and their spinsterhood. I have no reason to believe they failed either in kindness or in teaching, but they frightened imaginative children. When Stanley recovered he was transferred to St Stephen's school whose staff had been discreetly screened by auntie Abbie for youth and comeliness. She was rather proud that he went to a church school and let it drop more often than was strictly necessary. But he now went to school alone.

He was quite happy in isolation. His studious interests widened. His intelligence developed to such a degree that in one memorable week he overawed the neighbourhood. His auntie Gertie who worked on the telephone exchange in St Helens had sent him an ingenious instructional toy. There was a pack of charts with questions printed on the left and the answers on the right but in a random order. A chart was set into a frame wired to a battery. You plugged one free terminal into a small socket by the question and with another took a stab at the answer. If you were right a bulb lighted up and the company exclaimed with admiration. When one chart had been mastered it was replaced by another requiring greater learning. The complete pack encompassed the whole spectrum of human knowledge and auntie Abbie was understandably delighted when Stanley showed himself to have assimilated the lot in the course of a single morning. He scored a flash of light with each prod of the terminal. That might have been expected of him on chart 1. But the later charts caused him no greater difficulty; he answered without hesitation questions on the height of the dome of St Paul's cathedral and the voyages of Vasco da Gama. Then he rounded off his performance by rattling through the final chart intended for post-graduates, leaving the terminals in place and the bulb burning on the explanation of $E=mc^2$.

People came in from next door, Miss Bullock, a school teacher, who might be expected to have a special interest in a prodigy, and her brother-in-law, Mr Lamb, a police inspector, who arrived a minute or two later seeming vaguely suspicious that some infringement of the law might be taking place. They were astounded. When they had gone Stanley confessed that his store of knowledge was less massive than it might appear. He had deduced that for the electric circuit to work question and answer must always be in the same relative positions, whatever the chart. Having discovered these positions through knowing the answer to the simple conundrums on chart 1, he could light the bulb regardless of what the question might be or indeed without a chart in place.

Auntie Abbie and uncle Ben had come to accept that some of Stanley's conversation would go over their heads. They did not wholly grasp what he said, but they did glean that some prestidigitation had been practised on Miss Bullock and witnessed by the watchful Inspector Lamb. Uncle Ben announced that they could all be up a very nasty gumstick. They took the sensible course of refusing to hear any more of Stanley's explanation. They rebuked him for running down his own genius and auntie Gertie's kind present and required him to write her a letter of thanks. He was instructed as an afterthought not to mention his blitz-krieg but to imply a more plodding progress in case she might think him the kind of boy who would wolf down a whole chocolate bar at one go.

The Lambs and the Bullocks engaged our curiosity. Nine of them all adult lived in the four-room house. When they filed out en famille it was like watching the Mack Sennett film in which an endless procession of motor cars roll out of a garage hardly big enough to house one. On week mornings Frank Lamb, an older son, tumbled out first behind his smouldering Woodbine and coughed the length of Irene street to his wood yard at the far end. He was so punctual that people who wanted to rise at seven needed no alarm clock. Lights came on in bedrooms in the wake of his cough.

The Lambs supplied us with cracked eggs, produced at their pen and sold in prodigious numbers and at trifling cost to all the street and friends and relatives beyond. Their back yard and kitchen were full of egg boxes. Mrs Lamb, beady-eyed and beak-nosed, fluttered about the street carrying basins of cracked eggs. We wondered whether they were all produced cracked or whether they were laid sound and broken in the congestion and turmoil of the home. When Inspector Lamb was off duty he would be seen proceeding towards the allotments and would then be lost to view for several hours. We discovered that he repaired to one of his hen cotes and passed his leisure peaceably sitting on an oil drum with the door locked from the inside.

At the other side of auntie Abbie dwelt Harold Alderson, manager of the Temple street branch of Maypole Dairies, a thin bald man with sharp features and a forthright engaging manner which overcame the handicap of hailing from Halifax. He wore a tasselled apron down to his feet which made him look eight feet tall. He so towered above everything in the shop that he could be seen in fancy as a giant chess player who might lean over and move a customer like a piece on the black and white checkered floor. He personally delivered groceries to the doors of his neighbours and he conferred other bonuses, cheap broken biscuits, advertising balloons and tin yoyos and the loan for those who might find it useful of an instrument for writing prices on windows.

He also brought high drama, stories of altercations and attempted thefts and on one occasion of a close approach to insurrection. Long after the shop had been closed for the night at eight o'clock and the barred wooden gate locked across the porch an inspector from the company detained him with a series of trivial inquiries and, unable to discover any fault, commented that a pyramid of marmalade jars was too close to the edge of the counter. Harold demurred. The inspector demonstrated his point by brushing the jars to the floor. On hearing of this, auntie Abbie and uncle Ben tutted and shook their heads. Harold Alderson, encouraged by their sympathy, flushed with anger. 'If I hadn't heard the delivery lad come in the back door, I'd have taken my apron off and knocked him down,' he said. Mrs Alderson, a fat little woman who, like many females bred in the West Riding, had a round face and a tiny mouth, gave a cry of shock and repeated 'No, Harold. No.' She tugged at his sleeve as though there and then he might sail into the inspector. 'I would,' he said, brushing her off. 'If I hadn't heard the delivery lad come in the back door, I'd have taken my apron off and knocked him down.' 'No, Harold, no.' To her despair he repeated his threat half a dozen times then to introduce a little variation rearranged the order of the clauses, 'I'd have taken my apron off and knocked him down if I hadn't heard the delivery lad come in the back door'. By now auntie Abbie and uncle Ben had joined Mrs Alderson in pouring oil on the stormy waters though, as became neighbours, with less urgency and insistence. They did not actually speak but the sounds they made of shock and sympathy seemed to be having a calming effect when suddenly Harold reared like a jerked rope and announced that tomorrow he would throw the inspector through the plate glass window. Mrs Alderson wept. Uncle Ben nipped out to put the kettle on. Auntie Abbie asked us what we were standing about for.

We knew it would come to nothing. Passion in adults was not the prelude to action but a substitute for it. I suppose many who in those days enjoyed a small promotion paid for it by a lifetime of oppression from the person on the next rung up.

Irene street although unpaved was rather posher than our street. The boys and girls who on average were slightly older than us played together in a variety of quite organised and structured games. Some of them had gardens a couple of hundred yards away at the foot of the grazing ground of Brunshaw hill, and their play was altogether more mature and full of fancy than ours. At the centre of the group were the three Yates sisters whose father, Jack Yates, the publicity

officer of the Co-op, moved in elevated circles; on the piano
stood photographs of him in the company of the Bishop of
Burnley and of Arthur Henderson and Ramsay MacDonald.
He had diverted his talents to the service of the Church and
the Labour movement when his career as a comedian
crashed. At the time we knew him he would emerge from
the back gate and perform to the shame of his daughters
excerpts from the acts for which he had been hooted from
the boards. He had a wide mouth and a big red nose,
assumed a stoop and moved like a quick insect. Stanley had
the wit to respond to his jokes and a rollicking infectious
laugh which made all the other children laugh. He established
himself as a sort of partner and if he was not out Jack Yates
would come to the back gate for him. The Yates sisters, as
Sybil told me years later, compiled in a notebook a list of
girls to which two boys' names were added for gentle
character and conspicuous service. Stanley was one.

They admitted us to their allotment where their mother, a
stately lady, reposed in a hammock. It was she, they said,
who wrecked their father's career. In his courtship he had
not ventured to disclose his profession but she spotted his
name on a billboard and hastened to the theatre to see if it
could possibly be the same man. Behind the domed eyebrows and inside a choker collar as deep as a bucket it
clearly was. He was well embarked on a series of improper
jokes when he caught her eye. He froze. The curtain was
brought down. She allowed him to continue but only with
a cleaned-up act, for which his cheated and enraged audience
nearly lynched him. Henceforth the pulpit and the soap box
were safer platforms.

We were warned by the Yates girls not to be surprised if
some day we found the hammock swinging empty. Their
mother had a 'murmuring heart' and was not long for this
world. On inclement days when she was unable to repose in
the hammock she reposed on the sofa, reading out comforting thoughts from books of Christian or pantheistic quo-
tations while Jack scuttled round doing the housework on
his return from publicising the Co-op. Thanks perhaps to
his ministrations, Mrs Yates survived him by many years;
she was spared to pass the age of eighty.

Mabel the youngest sister had a circle of friends not everybody could see. Her favourite lived in one of the crystals of coloured glass scattered broken when builders left the row behind Irene street half finished. In the garden there were fairies. They came to a bower Mabel had built in a corner of the pond. We had not seen a bower before. It turned out to be a small hut constructed of interlaced branches and reinforced by a tin sheet which bore the fading picture of a huge teapot which was being stoked with Co-op tea by a little man on a ladder. Mabel said some people did not believe in fairies and if we didn't we could go away. But fairies did exist, she knew that and she knew better than us because she was nine and we were only six. Stanley demurred mildly to the effect that there were two of us who were six so the sum of our wisdom might be greater than that of a single person of nine, but when the line of argument was shifted he agreed that the age of observers was not decisively relevant. Mabel said she left grub for the fairies at night and it had gone by morning. We asked what sort of grub. She said liquorice allsorts. Could dogs perhaps have taken them? Stanley asked. No, dogs did not like liquorice allsorts. That seemed conclusive. Mabel said we could come again.

The fairies brought us into confrontation with the Reverend Rathbone who lived next door to the Yates in Irene street and rented the next allotment to theirs. He ministered to a small sect, the Free Church of England, who met behind an unpainted door in the middle of a block of small shops in Church street. He had a mop of carroty hair, matching spectacles and a freckled face and pallid hands which fluttered like a conjuror's. He spent much time up ladders and on top of his greenhouse, perhaps to keep us under surveillance and perhaps to enjoy an aerial view of the neat geometry of the paths which divided the flower beds. They were laid in brick to match his hair and spectacles. He was given to singing when aloft and he was fond of poetry. Each flower bed had its own piece of doggerel in poker-work which he declaimed to visitors from memory with scarcely a glance at the plaque.

The kiss of the sun for pardon,
The song of the birds for mirth.
One is nearer God's heart in a garden
Than anywhere else on earth.

It was a beautiful garden. He won prizes for his violas and
dahlias and was in anguish whenever the Yates girls brought
children with tennis balls or bows and arrows. Jack Yates
helped to keep the peace by taking part in a drag act in aid
of church funds on the tennis court which belonged to the
Reverend Rathbone's church and lay the other side of
Yates's garden. Jack and the church organist, Mr Doran,
played an exhibition match wearing headbands and long white
skirts as Suzanne Lenglen and Helen Wills. It went down
so well that it became an annual fixture. The Reverend
Rathbone reciprocated with evening visits to Yates's parlour.
He burst into prayer as readily as into verse. 'Word of
prayer,' he would call in the middle of a conversation,
'Word of prayer,' and drop on his knees. He asked nothing
of the Lord in his own interest but those on whom he called
down especial blessing seemed an eccentrically assorted
group: our brothers and sisters on sick beds, sailors at sea,
market gardeners and forestry commissioners. It transpired
that as a boy he had been apprenticed to a market gardener.
Forestry commissioners remained unexplained. When the
war came he would add 'our boys and girls serving King
and country' but that was the better part of a decade away
and not to be dreamt of.

But the Reverend Rathbone was suspected of a dark secret
which was never quite broached in conversation in the
parlour. He was known to be a collector of manure. He had
a rabid terrier called Ginger which he had trained to fly out
of the house and guard horse droppings in the interval it
took him to arrive personally on the steaming growling
scene with bucket and shovel. The horse muck was not
simply dug into the soil but converted into liquid manure in
a pit at the corner of the garden screened by heavy growth
and discovered by Joan Yates when she fell into it in
searching for a ball. The stinking slime that covered her
surely could not only be liquified horse muck. What else

went into it? The Reverend Rathbone dodged away from the subject, made a joke with fluttering hands and, still somewhat at bay, brought the conversation to a close in what had become the accustomed way. 'Word of prayer,' he called, and sank to his knees. Sailors at sea, market gardeners and forestry commissioners were remembered. The manure passed from the agenda.

The Reverend Rathbone liked to tease and he retaliated for the hinted suspicions by telling Mabel he would seduce her fairies. He was making a dell and they would forsake her bower for his dell. Stanley reassured her, turning scrutiny first to the word. Bower he had loyally permitted to pass without comment; dell was a fancy he would not accept. He repeated the word with a come-come sort of chuckle. Dell indeed. He soon had news for Mabel. The moss and seashells of the dell, he was able to assure her, had been abandoned by such of the bolder fairies as had ventured towards it. They had been alarmed out of their wits by the shriek and clatter of the Reverend Rathbone as he fell from his perch atop the greenhouse. He had fallen off the greenhouse? Through the greenhouse. The wind had got under his carroty mop, a wig as it turned out to be, and whirled it above the tree tops. He clutched after it and slipped and fell, crashing through the panes and smashing plants. The little people, fairies, elves, gnomes, fitches and even the hobgoblins had fled in panic. The dell would remain desolate until the end of time.

The account was well received by Mabel Yates; less so by the Reverend Rathbone when it reached his ears through a worried old lady who inquired about his own well-being and the damage to the tomato plants. The source of the story was discovered and protest made. Uncle Ben told Stanley that if he was going to invent libellous extravaganzas of that sort he would have to stop playing with Jack Yates. There was even so, he said, an essential difference: Jack Yates's jokes were fictional, Stanley's started from a living person and made him participant in grotesque events which were either wholly invented or grossly exaggerated. This in fact described, as Stanley noted, uncle Ben's own practice under any anxiety of proceeding at a single bound from

troublesome fact to catastrophic speculation. He used a style
of speech which incongruously combined colloquialism and
high-flown formality. On this occasion he began by outli-
ning the dignity and power of the Reverend Rathbone,
Bachelor of Arts, ordinand of the Church, soldier of Christ,
a prelate able to summon to his cause the Bench of Bishops
and Courts Ecclesiastic, august judicial bodies founded on
the bones of St Peter and presided over by a knotty-faced
little joker wearing a mitre who for two pins would go
through the lot of us like a dose of salts, banish us to eternal
darkness and leave us hanging from the thumb screws. Even
without recourse to clerical privilege the Reverend Rathbone
might inaugurate proceedings in the civil courts which
would award for so grievous a defamation monumental
damages beyond the purse of sultans and pirates, and in
default of payment he and mamma would be incarcerated at
His Majesty's pleasure for life or ninety-nine years whichever
was the longer.

Something of the sort anyway. It was several years before
we began to enjoy uncle Ben's style as a sort of fan club and
commit his best performances to memory. But the essentials
were there at this early stage, the volubility that encompassed
one disaster after another, the dark alarmed eyes and the
sawing hand.

One day when I was at Stanley's house one of the Yates
girls called to ask us out to play. He politely declined. When
she had gone he explained that devils incarnate were after
him. Was that their name? No, it was what everybody said
they were. They had threatened to do him in. He went pale.

The marauders were the numerous loosely-related children
of a verminous family who dwelt somewhere at the edge of
the woods. The grown members stank like goats. When
they were spotted boarding the tram at its terminus at the
foot of Brunshaw hill passengers already aboard would flee
through the driver's door. One of the family was so fat that
in boarding the tram she had difficulty in squeezing past the
rail on the platform and had to be thrust through the inner
door of the car with the sole of the conductor's boot.
Sometimes she stuck badly and the driver walked the length

of the car to ease her bulk through the frame while the
conductor pushed. In the end she could go suddenly like a
cork from a bottle, downing the driver and dogs in the aisle
and knocking askew passengers who had failed to escape.
She coarsely clapped hats back on the wrong heads. The
family was widely feared.

An advance party of two of its infants appeared and
watched from a distance when the Irene street children had
gone some way in digging a shaft to Australia on the
abandoned building site behind their homes. Stanley was
extremely interested in the project and was able from a
study of his encyclopaedia to warn his friends in good time
of the difficulties they might expect to encounter as they
approached the centre of the earth. More devils appeared,
no longer just the two infant girls but grown male demons
of three or four. They kicked the cinders back into the hole.
They were driven off. They came back in greater numbers
and then towards evening the whole coven of them arrived.
They proclaimed that digging would cease forthwith. One
boy singled out Stanley. He threatened to return and dispatch
him with his uncle's humane killer if he so much as went
near the hole again. Stanley contented himself with indoor
pursuits for a long time after that.

Spider Parker was a gangling lonely man who was always
agreeably surprised to be spoken to by a child. He bent
double, peering over his spectacles, and listened with professional concentration. He was a printer's reader, a cultivated man; he came from the South of England, rode a sit
up bicycle and listened to music. He never managed to
join in the general neighbourliness, but made forays at
establishing friendships. He invited people to hear his records. It was then noticed that he had a little wife about the
place. It was also noticed that she was petrified from the
moment the gramophone started to grind out its tune. If she
so much as breathed heavily he would flash his spectacles at
her. If she coughed he would shout 'We're trying to listen
to music, woman', angrily wind up the gramophone and
start again at the beginning. One evening when the Yates
family went over for a recital she sat taut, not daring to

breathe or even to raise her eyes from the floor. Suddenly the tension discharged itself in a single convulsion and she kicked the hearth tidy jangling across the tiles. She ran and was not seen for a week.

Spider repaired to his garden for peace. It lay besides the Reverend Rathbone's, no less beautiful, heavy in season with the scent of sweet briar and old-fashioned roses. In one corner he had an old hansom cab overgrown with Virginia creeper and mock orange blossom. He would retire to its shade and sit eating summer fruits from a rhubarb leaf. The allotments were still and peaceful on hot afternoons. The Reverend Rathbone took the breeze sitting on the top spar of his greenhouse, Mrs Yates swung in the hammock waiting for death, Inspector Lamb was agreeably locked up inside his hen cote. The town hummed in the distance, the birds and occasionally the Reverend Rathbone sang, the note of an engine rose and fell from the wooden shed opposite where Joe Abbott the dirt track rider worked on his bikes.

But Spider Parker's soul was not at rest. His passions seethed and boiled, anger and indignation griped his guts. Spider was a Bolshevik, not a disciplined party member but a wild revolutionary whose rebellion sprang from exasperation of the spirit. He could enjoy tranquility as he ate fruit from his rhubarb leaf only in those moments when he was visited by the sweet vision of the exploiting classes strung in thousands from the lamp posts.

Socialism had been for a time a bond between Spider Parker and Jack Yates. They lent each other books. Spider had supported Jack Yates' successful campaign to end the employment of aged inmates of the workhouse on making shrouds. But his forbearance in this friendship as in other matters soon failed. In a surge of exasperation he denounced Jack Yates' socialism as a hollow sham and the venerated leaders of the Labour party and the trade unions as traitors, double dealers, lackeys of the capitalists, Social Fascists and toadies of the King. These facts, he said, were 'well known'. They were not well known to Jack Yates. He was exceedingly surprised. It further transpired that besides reposing trust in traitors he had underestimated the opposition which he naively imagined to be Mr Baldwin and the Tories.

Whole unsuspected categories of class enemies now emerged: White Guard interventionists, right-wing deviationists, left-wing deviationists, mad dogs and Trotskyites, wreckers and saboteurs, tools of international finance and agents of revanchist capitalism, running dogs of the Chinese imperialists and unleashers of new wars. All had been smoked out into the open thanks to the vigilance of the party and the people. They had been unmasked and their machinations exposed.

Jack Yates had barely assimilated the information before his very vision of the socialist society was assailed. He had vaguely imagined it as a prolonged sort of Sunday school treat, maypole dancing and bicycling, ready ears for orators like himself and Ramsay MacDonald, Shavian quips and contraception, disarmament and free false teeth. This, he learned, was bourgeois romanticism. He must think in terms of tractor factories and hydro-electric schemes. It was hardly necessary to point out that having been misled by men who from early childhood had been traitors to the working-class movement, Jack Yates had inevitably in his own exertions played into the hands of the class enemy. The role of the Co-op was objectively reactionary, his campaign against shrouds a distraction from the struggle, his sermonizing as a lay preacher in the Church of England an opiate of the people. St Catherine's would be transformed in due course into a museum of atheism. As for the Reverend Rathbone, he would be shot.

Spider Parker stayed gentle and lonely for weeks on end. His outbursts were sporadic and always directed at one of three targets, his frightened wife, traitors to Socialism, and God. He hated God years before Graham Greene made it a fashionable pastime. Unable to come to grips with Him he turned his rage on to His vicar in Irene street, the unfortunate Reverend Rathbone. 'You bigoted buffoon,' he would yell over the back yard wall. 'You ranting sanctimonious hypocrite. You should be burned alive in your own pulpit.' The Reverend Rathbone wrung his conjuror's hands and lamented, 'Oh dear, oh dear'. Irene street deplored it. Spider Parker varied the chastisement, and one day hit an unseen target. 'You money-grubbing witch doctor. You should be sunk in your stinking manure tank where you've drowned half the dogs and cats of the neighbourhood.'

The Reverend Rathbone could find no voice to reply. Spider Parker perceived that he had struck a vital spot. 'He trembled,' he said in a singularly inappropriate figure, 'like a vampire shown a crucifix'. Later he settled for Shakespeare. The reverend 'started like a guilty thing surprised'. Other residents did not allow themselves to be drawn but there were those who, when the Reverend Rathbone knelt for a word of prayer and asked protection for market gardeners and forestry commissioners, silently and with a reproachful glance at the bowed ginger head added their Tabbies and Towsers.

The Reverend Rathbone made a peace offering. On her birthday he gave Mabel Yates a pet rabbit. When it died its corpse was placed in a coffin in the presence of witnesses and given a Christian burial. The Reverend Rathbone made a headstone, beautifully lettered, 'In Memory of Dilly, a Faithful Pal'.

My brother Eric started school early. Though robust, he was an angelic-looking child whose blue eyes gazed into a fairy story and filled with tears at its end. He continued to take to bed with him his family of stuffed toys and some nights to weep through nightmares from which he could not be awoken. He was good-natured and amenable, easily settled with a toy or crayons. He erupted without warning. As a baby in a high chair he had signalled the end of his meals by flinging what was left in his dish about the room. He did the same with toys when he had had enough of a game. My mother showed him how to put things back in their cardboard box. He learned to help her. She would set him up with something else to play with and go back into the kitchen, then presently the room would explode again and she would find him standing with the cardboard box in the middle of the subsided storm ready to help her put the things away. She never fathomed him.

His illnesses were like a puppy's. He would sink rapidly to the point, it seemed, of extinction and recover just as quickly. He laughed a lot. He gorged through Christmas Day, amiably defeating in the confusion of the revelry attempts to put the chocolates out of reach and to forestall a fourth helping of jelly, and at night when the Kerrys had gone he threw the whole lot back into the fire. The doused and blackened grate with smoke barely rising became through the years a private symbol of the end of Christmas.

He was accident prone, partly because he sailed into everything bald-headed. He fell downstairs at three trying to carry a large bedroom chair; its leg gouged a piece out of his cheek and left a permanent weal. He learned to bat not in the usual way of poking at the ball but by wild flailing which wrecked the wickets, brained fielders and finally shattered the bat beyond repair. His rocking horse he rode with such vigour that he was flung against a wall, taking the bridle and the horse's nose end with him. Other boys slipped off stones and got their feet wet in the river; he went under. Tree branches gave way under him. Dogs bit him. A cinder thrown on the rec, one of hundreds shied with little harm in brief battles among boys, split his head open. People gaped in horror as we ran home at the big stained patch spreading across the back of his blouse. His precipitancy caused most of his accidents but he suffered more than his share of what might have happened to anybody. He persisted in going on a roundabout in the park against my grandfather's caution, fell off and ran back and struck him. When they got home he was contrite. He said it was his bad luck he was hitting. His ease and high spirits enabled him to bear his bad luck without resentment until in his mid twenties he rode it out.

Art gives us experiences just beyond the range of our senses, ideas that cannot quite be grasped, images that disappear in the attempt to hold them, glimpses of an undiscovered country, fleeting indeed yet powerful enough to make the familiar world seem drab, so that a sense of disappointment is endemic in life. Children return with greater regret. My brother was transported further than most. At the end of a story he was unable for some time to get his bearings in the room. Coming out of the pictures, he had to be held by the collar to prevent him walking into a pram or under a car. He was enthralled by stories whether read from a book or told by my grandfather. He never interrupted. He never took exception as children often do to variations in a familiar tale and he seldom asked questions at the end. He continued to gaze at the fading characters and when he spoke all he said was 'Tell me again'. As the end of our story of Joseph approached he would begin to weep because of the death of Jacob and also because the closing of the book would sentence him, slow and reluctant, to a room where other people were sitting about as though they had been there all evening.

His other-worldliness and his exuberance put him beyond the reach of normal discipline. It was as though he was born knowing that everything in life is a game and that freedom consists in refusing to engage in other people's games under their rules. My mother who thought her own notions universal was baffled. It was like dealing with a child who did not understand language. He did not argue. He was not defiant. He simply did not comply. It was as though two games under different sets of rules were being played simultaneously on the same pitch. Once in company when he seemed to be moving towards eruption she sent him the warning signal in common use, a beam from narrowed eyes. He narrowed his eyes in response, then he opened them wide. He narrowed them and opened them. 'Big eyes, little eyes,' he said batting like an Aldis lamp. Children on the floor with him giggled and joined in. He was usually pleased with himself and I am sure on this occasion he felt he and his mother had taught everybody a good new game. There was no question of mocking her. It would not have been part of his good nature.

She made her stand, sensibly it seemed, not on abstract precepts which he seemed incapable of grasping but on the solid ground of the plantation. The plantation was the gently graded bank, six or seven yards wide, between the river and the recreation ground. It was grassed and planted with trees. Its purpose was ornamental. No access had been afforded but at intervals the railings had been bent apart and children squeezed through after balls or to play by the river. The rec keeper did not object but there was a slight feeling of trespass which no doubt fortified my mother in forbidding Eric to go on the plantation.

She told him he might be drowned. But he had already fallen in the river and touched the bottom; he knew it was too shallow to drown. He did not argue. She found him playing on the plantation.

She reproved him for disobedience and for grieving her. She mentioned grandpa Sephton's brother Jim who had broken his mother's heart. Eric had heard of him and readily contributed to the conversation anecdotes he knew. She headed him off and brought out another threat in place of drowning – pneumonia through wet feet. When she went out for him he was playing on the plantation.

She took him home and spanked him. She threatened him with fever from the germs which slid past in millions in the brown water of the river. She brought up the artillery. Next time his father would give him a thundering good hiding.

When she found him on the plantation a couple of days later he was so engaged in his game that she had to shout repeatedly to get his attention. He squirmed through the railings and fell in step. As they crossed the rec he broke into a trot. My mother, agitated by shouting and in despair at the unremitting conflict, imagined him of like mind and feared that in panic he was running away from home to hide in the hills. She caught him and asked where he thought he was going. He said he was going home quick for his thundering good hiding so he could get back to the plantation.

The good hiding passed like a heavy bombardment. In the quiet when men raise their heads again and the landscape slowly comes to life, there he was again on the plantation. In those days there were no psychologists to iron children out but a crone was brought to bear who had retired from regular Sunday school teaching but kept up moralizing as a hobby when she felt equal to it. She explained to us what conscience was and how we should know when we were going astray because of its warning voice. She offered examples of the voice of conscience in action and was encouraged by Eric's ready interest in the stories. Conscience we could think of as the still small voice, perhaps as a little man inside us who spoke when we were about to do anything wrong. 'Does he wear a top hat?' Eric asked. Her face contorted, but it was clear from his gentle eyes that he was not a venomous child but merely mentally backward. No, she said, he did not wear a top hat. But, she continued, Eric had such a little man inside him and when next he was tempted to go on the plantation the little man would speak in warning. She added that if ignored, the little man's voice would become quieter and quieter and some day might not

be heard at all. This seemed a false move, to install the
alarm and immediately say how it could be switched off.
But Eric did not notice, lost in contemplation of the story.
The lady announced that he was 'subdued'. She was given
tea and cake for her pains, which she repaid by counselling
us on her way out to be obedient to our mother while we
had her because one day, and we knew not the day nor the
hour, a dark curtain would come down and she would be
gone from us for ever.

It had been an afternoon heavy with symbolism. Eric
went out for a breath of fresh air on the plantation.

My mother marched him home and sat him opposite her
across the table. Did he remember the old lady who had
spoken to him? It was a rhetorical question; the smell of
liniment and old wardrobes still hung in the air. Did he
remember the little man? 'Yes,' Eric said, 'in a top hat'.
However accoutred, did he remember what the little man
did? He remembered. Then had the little man not spoken at
the plantation railings? Yes, he had, Eric said with a brighten-
ing smile and there had been quite a lively incident. He had
one foot through the railings when the little man spoke.
'You mustn't go on t' plant,' the little man said. Eric
withdrew his foot, then thought 'I will'. 'You mustn't,' the
little man said. 'I will,' Eric replied. 'You mustn't.' 'I will.'
'You mustn't.' 'I will' – his boot stepping in and out the
railings. Finally he made his decision. 'Against the little
man's voice?' my mother quavered. 'No,' Eric replied. 'I
said, "Right then, I'm not going on t' plant" and t' little
man ran round and shoved me in through t' railings.'

Mrs Corbett commended a cane, specifically to deal with
the matter of the plantation and in general to uphold good
order and discipline. She was the handsome woman from St
Helens, my grandmother's lifelong friend, who had come
through a hard life with a drunken and early deceased
husband and therefore felt herself qualified to offer advice.
'They're getting big now, you must have a cane,' she told
my mother as one might at some point in the cubs' growth
warn a lion tamer to keep a red-hot iron bar handy. She
herself had proved the value of the cane. The good hidings
given their sons by her drunken husband had been in

themselves beyond reproach but sporadic and unrelated to
any offence. The cane in her hand pointed the error and
stimulated the response. They jumped to. Through the years
she acquired the style of a hut corporal going round naming
blemishes and passing on immediately in the knowledge
that in her wake people would fall upon remedies. 'Archie,'
she would say looking not at my father but up 'one of the
curtain rails is split'. Or to my grandfather, 'Ted, the petals
are starting to fall from the fuchsia'. One day she came
rocking over the threshold and said, 'Donny, concrete the
step'. It was an absurd command. I knew the use of concrete
in the making of school yards and in the manufacture of
boots for swarthy chaps who were dropped to permanent
anchorage on the bed of the East River, but I had no notion
of working with it. Mrs Corbett's sons would have learned
at my age, chased out to the sand and cement with the cane
scuttering at their heels. Before she left she gave us all a
parting present, an apple and sixpence each to Eric and me,
a saw blade to my father and a cane to my mother. We
expressed surprise and gratitude. She hoped we would all
put our presents to good use. She personally hung the cane
by its crook over the corner of the mantlepiece. The next
evening when everybody was at chapel Eric took it down,
broke it up and threw the pieces on the fire.

People said he would be better when he went to school.
Mother registered him early and prepared the ground well.
He was keen to go and proud to be singled out for early
admission. She bought him a proper boy's school outfit and
delivered him to the headmistress. He found that after all he
did not care for school. Within half an hour he was home.

Mother took him back. This time he was not delayed by
the need to assess the place. She had hardly got back home
when she heard the front door opened behind her and there
he was in the hall. She reasoned with him. The teacher
offered him a model farmyard to play with if he would stay
and showed him the corner where he would have to stand
facing the wall if he ran away. He ran away. The doctor's
collector, an affable exhausted old man who happened to
call just when he arrived home, spoke of the value of
education to the working-class, mentioning such celebrities

as D.H. Lawrence and Ramsay MacDonald. A woman who had been a nurse tried to make clear the choice between on the one hand an unlettered life of ignorance and squalor and on the other a pensioned career in the warm offices of the Burnley Building Society or the Co-op. Eric accepted these counsels with an amiability that could have been mistaken for understanding. He continued to escape from school. He was threatened with the school board (truancy officer), the policeman, his father and God. He was begged not further to grieve his mother, the kind headmistress and Jesus. Mother against her own conscience gave him money for sweets as a bribe to return. She found him sitting on the window sill of the shop eating them.

There was an intermission. He was not yet required by law to go to school. Mother postponed the battle – with some self-censure because of the principle that anything disagreeable ought to be tackled forthwith. But I guess she was secretly glad to have him home again. The nature which so baffled her in moments of conflict was in the dailyness of life a foil to her own and a comfort. I think she found the place dull when he was not there, and I think my father was pleased to see him again waiting at the factory gate at dinner time.

Fulledge school was a sombre building like a prison. Eric in later years called it his Colditz. From the moment his incarceration began again his only object was to organize escapes. In the beginners' class he alone had seen it all before. At playtime he led half of them to freedom. The heavy gate of the boys' yard was locked. He led them out through the girls' yard. That gate was locked. He found his way out through the chapel; through the caretaker's boiler room; over the lavatory wall. The threats and promises which had failed before failed again. But now new elements appeared. Something was found he was good at – running races, which seems to have been given a thankful central place in the curriculum. Also he was beginning to enjoy the rewards of being a public figure known through the school and by repute to many parents. The arrival of corporation workmen to stick broken glass along the top of the high walls, though really intended to keep out trespassers in the evening, was

universally accepted as a desperate measure to contain the
inmates by day. Admiration and esteem were unbounded.
He was given sweets by children, some of the teachers
warmed to him, and in the natural way of things some of
the bigger boys started to knock him about. He asked me to
come and remonstrate.

He named a boy called Sykes. I knew the family. They
lived either in the UCP tripe shop on Lyndhurst road or
next door to it and they baked savouries which they sold
along the back streets at night. 'Hot torpedoes, hot meat
pies, hot meat and potato pies,' they sang, the voice rising
and lingering on its highest note on the middle syllable of
'potato'. You heard them coming and you heard them go
until the voice became indistinct and lost in the closer
sounds of the fire and the gaslight. It was the son of this
distinguished family that I waylaid on request.

Eric was not present at the encounter but expressed
satisfaction and offered further names for assault. Had they
all attacked him? Not at all, none of them had. It was not a
question of retaliation nor even of pre-emptive strikes. They
were just boys whom he thought a good hiding would suit
rather well. I felt something of my mother's consternation
faced by a child who was either wholly amoral or not
compos mentis. You didn't paste folk for nowt, I said. But
Sykes, he said, had been pasted for nowt. Sykes, I said, had
been pasted for pasting him. Sykes, he said, had not pasted
him, not that Sykes, not the hot torpedo Sykes, it was
another Sykes.

I knew of no precedent. A pasting could not be withdrawn. Some reparation was due to torpedo Sykes, in justice
and also in case he found the readiest redress in giving Eric
the pasting he had not given him but had himself been
pasted for. When cornered and calmed Sykes proved to have
a clear mind. He had an older brother, he said, who would
rectify matters by pasting me but it would be a question of
finding the occasion. He had now left school and was
working in the business so he was up to his elbows in
dough or chopping mounds of onions at those hours of the
day when he might otherwise ambush me. In the evenings
he carried round the torpedoes on his head and could not

risk setting down his steaming tray under the noses of the
dogs at his heel for long enough to engage in a bout of
fisticuffs. It was useless to go on looking for a legalistic
solution. Eric resolved it in his broader way by taking Sykes
home and inviting him to choose a toy from one of our two
cardboard toy boxes – which happened to be mine.

They finally induced Eric to stay at school by allowing
him to sit by whomever he wished. He chose a pretty child,
June Bromilow, and brought her home to tea. She was a
young lady of good family. Her father was the manager of
Burnley football club and they lived in one of the large
houses in Woodgrove road which overlooked the river and
the rec from a crest of parkland. I was released from school
later than the infant classes and when I got home she was
installed at the table. Her mother had given permission, our
mother had got out the Sunday table cloth and crockery and
set a tea of unusual delicacy. The young people carried on a
confident and laughing conversation. Eric passed the jam
with savoir faire.

It was an event of such novelty that it was spoken of long
afterwards. Nobody came to tea on weekdays and few
except relatives at any time. Simply to bring someone from
school was unheard of. Only a boy who was careless of
ridicule outside the home and of teasing within would have
dreamt of bringing a girl. In the immediate locality boys
and girls seldom played together, and segregation was
strengthened by an arch and teasing 'Wasn't the girl I saw
you with at Brighton' attitude often assumed by adults. My
grandfather sang a song from his childhood:

> Hop, hop, hop to the butcher's shop,
> I dare not stay no longer.
> For if I did my Ma would say,
> 'You've been playing with the girls down yonder.'

He would sing it with a wagging finger and a raised
eyebrow. It was guyed and comical but with an element of
mockery I would not have cared to be the target of. In
speaking at home of the children at school I never mentioned
the two I liked best, both girls.

I was given the desk next to Hetty Harrison in a reorganisation of the class. Boys usually sat in one half of the room
and girls in the other but there were different systems. You
could be seated in blocks representing different houses, the
symbol of which was a plain coloured tin brooch for the
other ranks and one with the word Monitor or Captain for
the leader. You could also be arranged in order of merit like
a league table, though there seemed to be no certain rule
whether the declension should start off across the width of
the back row or down the length from back to front.
Sometimes the top scholar was actually put at the front of
the class, a sort of pole position on a starting grid. You
could never tell. In a classroom not visited before you had
to fall back on gross physical characteristics to distinguish
the intellectuals from the thickheads.

It was not a competitive system that brought me to sit by
Hetty Harrison. The class was simply seated in alphabetical
order, with the agreeable effect that our response when the
attendance register was called rippled like a cracker across
the rows with a brief misfire at empty desks. I found it
pleasant to sit by Hetty, and after a couple of weeks I spoke
to her. She responded quick and bright as though she had
been waiting. She was fair with a sharp face and dark lashes

which made her look as though she had just ceased weeping
and was about to laugh. I noticed her hand on the desk and
the fall of her hair when she bent to write and her quick tidy
habit of popping pencil and ruler into a draw-string bag.
She wore cotton dresses gone pale and limp and with the
bloom of wear upon them. I had never observed a girl so
closely before. She took me in her stride. Her mother sent
me a sweet, which revealed to me how secret I for my part
had kept the affair at home. They lived in a poor street
alongside Fulledge chapel and the age span of the family was
large. On Armistice Day when we sat with heads bowed
during the two-minute silence she wept for her brother who
was killed in the war. That must have been at least five
years before she was born.

She copied my sums. Usually she took in what she needed
in an artful glance which encompassed the window and the
ceiling. When my hand or blotter concealed the figures she
leaned by way of persuasion against my shoulder. One day
she copied a sum I had got wrong. The teacher laboured the
detective logic and caned us both. Hetty wept. When playtime came and the teacher went out of the room Hetty
rounded on me and gave me a good hiding. I saw that
relationships with girls were not as simple as people might
think.

It was nothing to what lay in store on the other side of
the aisle. Ruth Heaton, only one vowel away in the alphabet
and therefore no more than a couple of desks distant in the
classroom, nevertheless belonged to a different world. She
was an artiste, and thus felt constrained to perform the
alarming and astonishing antics that years later I learned to
recognise as the normal behaviour of show business. She
went to elocution lessons where she had learned a poem.
The teacher asked her to recite it to the class. Ruth struck
off in an accent that was nothing like her ordinary speech
and far beyond the 'swanky' accent of the teacher. It was as
though a cat had barked. Some children sniggered, some
chortled, most of us sat amazed. At the line 'Oh, it must
have been an angel' Ruth allowed her head to fall back a
little, closed her eyes and circled her arms upwards and
outwards. Several uncouth boys guffawed, kicked their desk

irons and wiped their snotty noses on their jersey sleeve.
Thus set off, the pent-up amazement of the class broke out
into an unrestrained laugh. Ruth awakened from her vision
of the angel to see the other children rocking about and the
teacher skipping up the aisles slapping anyone within reach.
Poor Ruth sat down with her face in her hands. I was sorry
for her because she had not asked to recite and after all we
knew nothing about elocution. When the bell went I said to
her that it was a good poem and well rendered. She instantly
revived.

'Oh, it's wonderful of you to say so,' she said, half in her
elocution voice. 'I was terrible. But how sweet'. She
stretched her arm to touch my sleeve, smiled, then threw
back her head and performed one of those laughs of great
duration by which celebrities on chat shows contrive to
show off their capped teeth. It was even more startling than
the angel, though recognisably from the same stable. I had
no notion of the gratitude with which an artiste will repay a
word of encouragement from the lay public. Ruth gave me
sweets, she sent me billets doux in class, she waylaid me
near the school gate, not in the sidling way some girls
might but stepping to a clear space on the pavement as I
approached, frankly waiting. She was a happy child and
her exuberance was part of her nature rather than of the
affectations she had learned. These rather died away as time
passed and in ordinary conversation she spoke like anybody
else. She confined her elocution to the elocution class. Even
so, she was different from others. We complied and hid our
feelings; she was open and expressive. We were dourly
serious; she was a joker. Her first billets doux, folded and
passed under desks with conspicuous secrecy, were like
ordinary greeting cards with a flower crayoned in the corner
and a few words written big. Always! Till Eventide! Good
Morning! She progressed to comment. Like Your Jersey!
Who Cut Your Hair! Ha, Ha, Laughed the Little Pig! She
also did some rather good drawings and she brought me
from her uncle who worked in a mill several yards of
burning band, a sort of hollow-stemmed string which would
glow and smoulder without going out.

I liked her but I was embarrassed to be seen with her, not

because of her style and originality, which I rather admired, but because of her boots. They were of ruddy brown leather and knee length. What was wrong with them was that nobody else wore that kind. Her spectacles and auburn hair were also unusual but you could get used to them and like the way she looked. It was part of her. The boots were separate like the elocution but more persistent and conspicuous. Boys could wear nothing different from others without attracting scorn. Girls were allowed slightly more latitude but not as far as I was concerned in footwear. The Achilles heel of my tolerance was in boots. Because of my father's trade I had suffered the long shame of never wearing clogs and I had recently had an appalling experience with a new Sunday pair of shoes. They were neat and, as I argued, unmanly. My father showed me the box. It said boys' shoes. And then in Sunday school, my head bowed in prayer, I had seen resting on the spills of the chair in front of me an identical pair worn by the minister's daughter.

When I saw Ruth's boots waiting I took to darting down side streets rather than accompany them in the public gaze to school. She brought her little sister to head me off. I varied the route. I sneaked to school early. I went late and dashed in at the last moment. The Misses Heaton were delighted by the sport. I know how the fox feels when he hears the jolly laughter of the hunt. They advanced up Lyndhurst road to close down my options. One day they were waiting outside my house. I was paralysed. I did not dare to look over my shoulder lest my grandfather was already at the parlour window with raised eyebrows. In the desperation of the moment I found myself performing a gesture quite out of character and rather, I suppose, in the style of the elocution class. I gathered Ruth and her sister in outstretched arms and breezily wafted them out of sight round the corner shop of E.S. Cubbins High Class Boot and Shoe.

Somebody with a nimbler mind might have improved the occasion by turning Ruth's thoughts towards a change of footwear. But there would have been no point. People had only one set of clothes for school and they were made to last for years. They were part of your identity. I can remember some people by their jerseys even though I can no longer remember their features. Ruth was landed with the unfortunate boots for every winter until they dropped to bits or her sister's feet grew big enough to fit them. It would have been unkind of anybody to have criticised them. For me, clumping along in boots heavily studded with hobnails as a feeble substitute for clogs, the very neurosis about footwear which made Ruth's boots appalling also made it an absolutely impossible subject ever to think of mentioning. And so because the blemish was ineradicable I sought to escape her company which I enjoyed. Fortunately she was robustly determined that I should continue to enjoy it whether I like it or not.

I begged her in their own interest not to come into Hinton street again. Disease was sweeping through the houses of a most infectious kind; the inhabitants were dying like flies and even passers-by dropping like ninepins. What disease? asked Ruth. Scarlet fever, I said. That's nowt, Ruth said. And as people sometimes invoke a foreign translation to reinforce a point she added in her other language, 'Absolutely nothing'.

Everybody knew, I said, that scarlet fever was nowt and absolutely nothing, but that was only the beginning. There were other diseases much more infectious to passers-by and too frightful to mention in front of her sister. They both laughed. Come on, Ruth said, she bet I didn't even know their names. She underestimated the medical education of Nonconformist hypochrondriacs. Diptheria, I said, meningitis, scrofula, rabies, yellow fever, distemper, whooping cough, bubonic plague, swine fever, foot and mouth disease and hydrophobia to name only those diagnosed up to midday. They laughed all the way to school. Ruth removed her spectacles to wipe her eyes.

These fanciful kinds of exchanges increased our friendship. They also served to strengthen a note of mockery which had been slightly present from the start. Ruth sent me folded notes which proved to be blank. She sent some with nonsense verse and one with the lines of an In Memoriam from a newspaper.

He did not know he could not stay.
God said, 'Time's up'
And whipped him away.

Some of the notes no longer came privately by the shortest
route but were passed like an office memo round a list of
names. It transformed my position. I was no longer a private
recipient but the butt of a public joke. Moreover I had
already been spotted by other boys traipsing to and from
school with Ruth's boots and her sister, and it could only be
a matter of time before the scandal came to the teasing
notice of my grandfather. I conveyed something of the
burden of my concern to Ruth without mentioning the
boots. Yes, she said, but what people didn't know was that
her sister was not on her way to or from school. I said I
knew that, she was too young. But, asked Ruth, did all
these people know where her sister was going? I confessed
they didn't. Well, she would tell me, but there was no need
to spread it round everybody, was there? I said there wasn't.
Her sister was looked after by a lady in Plumb street in the
afternoons when their mother was at work, and she was
glad I had mentioned it because she wanted me to help her
collect her sister after school.

By the time I grasped that the stream was taking an
unexpected course I was already swept out to sea. I was
never quick to spot artful motive and I always felt an
obligation, often reluctant, to do what was asked of me.
This one at least would be quickly discharged, and it lay in
a safe direction. Ruth and her sister walked two sides of a
triangle to waylay me on my way to school. The third side
was the direct route to their home by the cricket field and
away from Lyndhurst road where my pals trooped home
and my grandfather might lurk. When we collected the
sister Ruth cut back towards Todmorden road, which was
still in the safe direction but a longer way round. I asked
why. She said to go to St Catherine's. She spoke with some
surprise as though it was something she thought I knew. I
said you couldn't go to church on weekdays. She said you
could. I said it wouldn't be open. She said it was. Her sister
saw the promised visit was in jeopardy and her lip began to

quiver. The last thing I wanted was a scene in the street. They would find out when they got there and that would be the end of it. Nobody went into our chapel on weekdays except the caretaker. The front door was permanently locked except on Sunday and the caretaker had taken to locking the back door behind him since my brother had used the chapel as an escape route from school. St Catherine's, I had no doubt, would be likewise locked. Ruth grasped the iron ring of the handle in both hands and opened the door.

I had never been in the Church of England before and I stood in some awe getting used to the semi-darkness. I imagined from the columns and arches that it was a very ancient building. Light from a high window fell on the altar, faded flags brought back from battle hung near the roof, the names of the dead were chipped in the wall.

Ruth switched on the light in a side chapel which she said was their Sunday school. It was a shock that the Sunday school should be in the church and also that it should be so untidy, like a play room, with drawings stuck on the wall and the chairs facing in different directions. I rather liked the place. It turned out that a few children called on their way home from school. I took to going with them, with a certain sense of secret vice and trespass. One afternoon the

vicar, the Reverend Harry Battye, approached when I was
about to leave. I stood more or less to attention expecting
that he would require an explanation. He laid on my head a
hand in a big glove of silver fur and passed on.

A double life on that scale could not conceivably be
concealed for long. Out of the blue Mrs Appleton threatened
to blow my cover. She was a foreign element in the drama,
a substitute in class while our own teacher was away ill. She
was married which teachers generally were not, she was
grey, she was nasty not in the superior manner of teachers
but in a fierce and plaintiff domestic way. She it was who
bowed her head at the name of Jesus; she was a Roman
Catholic. She intercepted one of Ruth's billets doux on its
way to me round the class. What it said I do not know but I
have no reason to think it could have been exceptionable and
it may well have been one of the blanks. Mrs Appleton
spoke in anger. 'My word, I'd set about my children if I
caught them at this kind of thing. I'd set about them with the
stick.' She flashed her dark eyes about the class, at Ruth, at
me, at each of the addressees on the circulation list. 'The
headmaster is going to hear about this, and some of your
parents.' She placed the note in her official folder which contained the accounts for the milk money and contributions to
the Yorkshire Penny Bank.

So that was that. From the fear of being teased by my
grandfather I had slipped step by step into a life so deceitful
as to be the subject of criminal record. I did not doubt that
Mrs Appleton would know about and report on my visits
to the Church of England. I decided that when charges were
preferred I would make a clean breast of it and confess
everything, including having been blessed by the vicar.

Nothing so drastic proved necessary. The weeks passed.
Our teacher recovered. Mrs Appleton left, her file undis-
closed, her can of worms unopened. The church palled. I
went there just occasionally with the children from the class,
not often, but one day we met my grandfather. He stopped
and talked and made everybody laugh. Ruth responded to
him well, two performers together. When I got home I told
him where I had been going. He told me about the church

school he had attended as a boy, then he held up a cautionary finger as though about to turn to graver aspects. But the pause was for recollection. He searched his memory and recited in the sing-song of his childhood passages from the Catechism, words of the tattered flags and vaulted arches. 'I believe in the Holy Ghost; the Holy Catholic Church; the Communion of Saints; the Forgiveness of Sins; the Resurrection of the Body; and the Life Everlasting.' It pleased him to remember the whole recitation.

I said that Ruth to whom he had been talking recited; she was a student of elocution. He said she had a well schooled voice. There was a pause then, like a penitent who leaves to last what lies most grievous in his heart, I said she sometimes wore funny boots. Funny boots? he asked. Yes, I confessed, funny boots. In fact she had been wearing such boots when we met him. He said he had not noticed; all the children seemed well turned out in every respect and very suitably shod.

One day in the autumn of 1931 we heard Jack Yates had an immensely important personage in his parlour in Irene street. The Yates girls spoke as though their father had captured an elephant, and indeed the man in the front room was very large and affable and eating buns. The girls and some of the adults addressed him as uncle Arthur. He was the universal uncle of the Labour party, Arthur Henderson, M.P. for Burnley, Leader of the Opposition, lately Secretary of State for Foreign Affairs, a leading light in the League of Nations, a Wesleyan and teetotaller. We gathered he had come to engage the powers of darkness. We were given yellow paper badges with his name in red to wear as witness of our support.

By the age of seven we were clear about who was on the Lord's side: Methodists of all kinds, Lloyd George, Burnley football and cricket clubs, missionaries, cowboys in white hats and now, for a few weeks above all, uncle Arthur. His opponent in the election, Vice Admiral Gordon Campbell, V.C., was so clearly a symbol of all that was to be deplored that it was incomprehensible that anybody might vote for him. This was the first general election after Ramsay MaDonald in financial crisis formed the National government in alliance with Conservatives and some Liberals, thereby moving his own party to adopt and ever after to adhere to the Spider Parker view of his life and works. His photograph disappeared from Jack Yates' piano top. The anguish of the realignment dominated the election nationally but in Burnley because of the character and record of the candidates, the campaign came to centre on the issue of peace. Jack Yates, holding forth from a soap box which was carried from street end to street end by a dwarf, found lines to quote from a recent hymn with which to torpedo the seadog.

> Far-called, our navies melt away;
> On dune and headland sinks the fire;
> Lo, all our pomp of yesterday
> Is one with Nineveh and Tyre!
> Judge of the Nations, spare us yet,
> Lest we forget, lest we forget.

The electors of Burnley were not likely to forget about war. The names of brothers, sons and husbands ran to thousands in the memorial book in Towneley Hall. But they did not share Jack Yates' notions about the maintenance of peace. Pressed to choose they had more faith in guns than in the Lord and the League of Nations. The vice admiral sank uncle Arthur.

It was the only time in these years that the wash of wider events reached our doorsteps. We knew of the 'empire overseas' whose products posters asked us to buy, and of Germany whose cheap toys and clocks were marked 'Made in Wurttemberg' to disguise where they had really come from. We had of course a notion of darkest Africa where the missionaries plied their trade and of the America of the cinema but these were, like the places of fairy stories, more of the imagination than of the outside world. Australia we knew of. Two aviators, Scott and then Jim Mollison, went wobbling off there in the wake of Amy Johnson. And by getting up to the wireless at three o'clock you could hear the Test match from Australia, though the commentator's voice was often drowned out by a hiss and roar which we took to be the rise and fall of intervening seas and oceans. Australia was infinitely distant.

What was happening unheeded by us in the great world? I looked up a list of the events of 1931 compiled by the BBC at the time. What apparently commanded attention were such events as the tour of South America by the Prince of Wales, a new motor speed record by Captain Malcolm

Campbell, the appointment of a new Dean of Canterbury, the opening of Whipsnade zoo, new plays by Somerset Maugham and Noël Coward. In this chronicle of the year there is no mention of Germany, Russia or the United States nor indeed of any other foreign country except India as the recipient of a new capital and Australia as the destination of aviators – with just one exception. In September Japan, in the cautious phrase of the archivist, 'took military action' in Manchuria.

We lived in a little inward-looking community, in a little inward-looking country. And we lived at a time, before the forebodings of the 'thirties began, when people looked back. What they looked back to was the eternal summer of 1913 when it seemed that peace would endure and prosperity would grow for ever. The aspiration of the 'twenties, it has been noticed, was expressed in words of return: reconstruction, restoration, recovery. The Great War was still seen not as the end of an age but as an interruption. The biggest industries, coal and textiles, reached record production in 1913, which would have been exceeded the next year and must surely be reached again when things returned to normal. Britain had financed and armed itself and massively supplied its allies through four years of war. So powerful an economy could surely not fail to revive.

Patience was the virtue of the 'twenties. Things took longer than might be supposed. Even the weather had not settled down again from the pounding it suffered from the heavy guns. A patient thought of the time remained in my father's mind for use on the rare occasions through the years when he expressed an opinion. When he was old and dependent on the pension he was against accepting an increase; it should be deferred, he thought, 'until the country gets back on its feet again'.

Restraint and good will seem to have been a characteristic not only of the five million who returned from the war, trained in waiting and grateful to be alive, but of the country as a whole. A.J.P. Taylor, not a complacent historian, writes: 'National loyalty transcended class consciousness except for a small minority, and it is possible in this period to write the history of the English people rather than the history of the exploiting classes . . . This was the best time that mankind, or at any rate Englishmen had known: more considerate, with more welfare for the mass of people packed into a few years than into the whole of previous history'.

The war cast over these years of my early childhood the shadow of a great bereavement. The sentiments of the war writers published in 1929 and 1930, of sorrow and infinite regret, were echoed in common speech, usually without the asperity. Contrition was felt about those who had suffered or died or lost, and expressed in gentleness towards others and an awareness, new in the world, of the value of every life. Children of my generation were the beneficiaries, cherished, protected and spared harshness. They were both seen and heard. They became the centre of the home.

There is another thing. Time was slow in those patient years. Outside the factories it still moved to the beat of a grandfather clock or the plod of horses' hooves. Days were long. The old especially had plenty of time, to light their pipes or to weigh out sweets in their corner shops or to accost us, as they did, for the pleasure of being known and knowing us. Their greetings often took the form of crusty rebukes. If we sauntered about the rec not actually engaged in a game old men also sauntering would demand 'What art thou doing?' 'Nowt,' we would reply. 'Well, stop it,' they would say, not raising their voice, trudging on, hardly looking at us, with affection. It was a good time to be a child.